Box 44, Monrovia
by Nona Freeman

THE STORY OF GLADYS ROBINSON

BOX 44, MONROVIA

by Nona Freeman

Hazelwood, Mo. 63042
Second printing, June, 1983
Third printing, November, 1984

ISBN 0-912315-09-1

Cover Photography by Peter Carr
Cover Design by Tim Agnew

All Scripture quotations in this book are from the King James Version of the Bible unless otherwise identified.

Printed in the United States of America.

WAP WORD AFLAME® PRESS
8855 Dunn Road • Hazelwood, Mo. 63042

Mary Ann England

Box 44, Monrovia

by Nona Freeman

THE STORY OF GLADYS ROBINSON

Preface

Our first meeting was a Spring Missionary Convention at DeRidder, Louisiana, in 1947, not long before Gladys Robinson left for Liberia.

I have tracked her for the past six years through conversations with her friends and letters from them and her diaries and letters to her children. I could not have found her again without their gracious assistance. She has emerged loving, brave, and thoroughly human with a swath of refreshing humor that softened her total dedication.

Excerpts from her diaries and letters, only slightly edited or rearranged for clarity, express Gladys uniquely. Where the letters ended I have relied on word of mouth reports and memories that can be tricky and elusive. There may be confused facts or happenings omitted; still, the lady is there, warm and lovely enough to keep me entranced and scribbling away to the end in many odd and even uncomfortable conditions.

Brother A. R. Williams was embarrassed at her funeral because there wasn't a black car available. He led the procession in a coral-colored Mercury with his face a deeper color. Dorothy Williams said, "If she could peek, she would be laughing!" A delightful summary of Gladys.

Though Maheh has joined Beajah and other missions in oblivion, Bomi Hills is still a strategic gospel center. Building Bomi was a distinct achievement, but the deepest significance of her ministry was the swing away from the maternalistic avenue of mission service to basic evangelism.

She was a torch with a brief flaring and burned out quickly after pointing to a new direction. A true pioneer!

Nona Freeman

Special Thanks
to
Ransom Rambo
for his
unique illustrations

Contents

Contents

Foreword

There were probably forty people present in the little storefront home missions church at the foot of 27th Street in Moline, Illinois, in the fall of 1951. It was a special service, a missionary from Africa was present. A fourteen-year-old boy sat in awe as his pioneer preacher Daddy introduced the saintly missionary lady, Gladys Robinson. The stories she told, the need she shared, and the burden that she transmitted kindled a strange fire in the bosom of this preacher's boy that he was somehow never able to extinguish.

As that boy grew to manhood, the life and ministry and sacrifice of this great handmaiden of the Lord had a profound influence on his life. That fire consumed all other ambition and inevitably drew him to Africa.

Many are the times he has looked into Box 44 in the old Post Office in Monrovia, Liberia, and received strength, and inspiration as well as support for him and his family. I believe as you look into the inspiring pages of "Box 44", you will feel a profound inspiration and a warmth that may spark a flame in your life that will broaden the horizons of your vision of the work of a missionary like Sister Robinson as well as a need of a lost world as her life did in mine.

Samuel Latta
Missionary to Liberia West Africa 1965-1969
Presently missionary to
Zimbabwe Southern Africa

Chapter One

OUT OF THE SHADOWS

The attention span of a little girl is kin to a butterfly flitting from one blossom to another. One Sunday morning, the interest of a small dark-haired girl was snagged by something in her devout Baptist grandfather's sermon. Strange feelings twisted her heart and Gladys joined others at the old-fashioned mourners bench without understanding why she cried so hard. Then, along with paper dolls and childish games, that first touch of God on her heart was forgotten.

Gladys Elizabeth Cox was born May 17, 1907 in the rural community of Ozark, Illinois, the youngest of Betty Elizabeth and John Allan Cox's four children. She was a quicksilver child with a sunny disposition who could swing swiftly from a trill of laughter to obstinate wilfulness. Growing up years added intensity of feeling which brought both a deep capacity for love and a vulnerable heart.

Seventeen-year-old Gladys married her childhood sweetheart, Garrie Everett Ross, in 1924 with rosy dreams of "living happily ever after." By the time

Marie Evelyn was born in 1925, this union dulled to the hurting gray of blasted dreams and dissolved in 1927 just before the birth of her only son, Allan Loree.

Wedding bells and another hope for happiness came with Laban Carter Campbell in 1928. Carmen Elizabeth joined the family in 1930 bringing more joy. But, Carmen was only five years old when Carter died, and the world of Gladys caved in on her again.

Survival was the next chapter. She loved her children fiercely and regardless of passing time and their status in life, they would forever be her "precious babies"! A cousin, Anna came to baby-sit and she worked as waitress, telephone operator or whatever jobs were available.

Leo Robinson, a widower with three children, became her partner in 1939. No doubt she accepted him hoping for a way out of life's lonely perplexity. Her expansive loving heart opened to his daughters Jackie, Sue and Barbara, though this marriage was on the shaky side of compatability from the start. The vacuum was not filled, only rearranged.

July, 1940, someone invited a thoroughly disillusioned Gladys to a tent meeting in Glendale, Illinois. The fiery preacher was Raymond Yonts, father of Jack Yonts, the present Home Missions Director of the United Pentecostal Church. She listened entranced as the powerful message driven by God's Spirit pinpointed her life of heartache, sin and vain search for happiness.

"He's talking to me!" she thought, "Just to me!"

An unbearable longing for peace and pardon engulfed her. She was not conscious of running to the altar, but when she found herself there, deep racking sobs came from the depth of a soul that seemed beyond comfort. Suddenly, a soft edge of peace touched her and slowly spread its benign flow over the once tortured heart. Forgiven! The assurance was overwhelming. Tears fell again, but these were different, more like the benediction of a gentle rain.

Those praying around her urged, "Press on! Reach for the infilling of the Spirit."

She wanted only to bask in the glow of forgiveness and savour that amazing calm in her inner being. The voices were insistent, "Praise the Lord! He wants to fill you with the Holy Ghost!" She began obediently to worship and was blessed. Someone leaned over and said, "You have stammering lips—that is the Holy Ghost!"

She returned home that night with new found peace, though there was a question in her mind about the Holy Ghost. Early the next morning she took a Bible, heretofore barely used, and made a diligent search of the Scriptures on the subject. About the time she was fully convinced that the evidence of the Holy Ghost was a full language given by God and unknown to the recipient, Brother and Sister Yonts arrived, sent by the Lord to pray with her.

They went to a wooded area for prayer to eliminate possible distractions. On a carpet of grass under a beautiful tree, Gladys was born of the Spirit with clear utterance of an unknown tongue and was given a commissioning burden that would direct her for the rest of her life. She saw a dazzling light at the top of the large oak tree, in the center of shimmering radiance the head and shoulders of Jesus was briefly visible. The vision faded and in its place were mud huts with palm thatch roofs, scantily clad black women and naked babies. They reached for her out of dire need. The scene changed and she saw herself ministering to them and praying for their dusky little one. She knew then; one day she would go to the land of mud huts, but she confided only in her pastor, no one else. Brother Yonts baptized her in the Name of the Lord Jesus.

Leo first made a move toward the Lord then retreated. He bowed out of her life amicably, having no desire either to walk the new road with her or to hinder her in the way she chose to go.

A year later when missionary Peter Jensen spoke at the church in Carterville, Illinois, he paused and said, "Someone in this church will be a missionary to Africa.!"

Gladys whispered "I hope it isn't me." But in her heart she *knew*. She moved to Nashville, Tennessee in 1942, while the church was still worshipping in a tent on 51st and Delaware Avenues. Sometimes she would phone her friend Louise Dugan and say, "I must go out and work for the Lord. Will you go with me to knock on doors?" Louise dropped whatever she was doing and they went, often walking up and down the streets of Nashville giving out tracts and witnessing to whomever would listen. As her natural intensity firmed in dedication to God she sought eagerly for more avenues of service—delighted in teaching Sunday School (her class was called the Bereans) and regular services at a nearby T.B. sanatorium.

An ever-increasing burden for the lost took her back to her "Jerusalem," the rural community in Ozark, Illinois where she was born. Farmers, relatives and friends crowded the one-room school each evening to hear the fervent evangelist, once a pupil in that school. Here Gladys, the preacher was launched, sponsored by Raymond Yonts and backed by musician teen-aged daughter Carmen and prayer-warrior friend, Frieda McNew. World War II still raged in the summer of 1944. Dim light filtering from unshaded windows revealed many horse-drawn wagons outside and few cars, for gas was rationed, tires and spare parts for repairs were scarce. The one commodity in abundant supply was the Spirit of God flowing freely and transforming many lives. A church was born out of the revival that lasted several weeks. When crowds outgrew the school, they transferred to a tent and later, a rented building. The presbyter of the area, Brother Bennie Jones of Anna, Illinois, advised her to continue the work. She didn't feel qualified to pastor so agreed IF he would be pastor, she would be his assistant. The church prospered under her leadership and is still a lighthouse for the name of Jesus today.

All that dedication and determination may sound grim, but, for balance Gladys was graced with a wide streak of hilarity. Infectious laughter or mischevious pranks came easily. Such as the time she disguised herself with grotesque teeth and weird clothes and followed a nervous young preacher and his wife around patting them on the shoulder and asking silly questions.

Her friends thought 'another joke' when she announced her call to Africa, especially since she was so fearful of anything in the creepy-crawly class.

"Africa!" they hooted increduously, "You're so afraid of bugs'n worms'n spiders—what about snakes? Plenty of them over there! You'll never make it!"

They didn't realize the secret soul-searching agony, prayers and tears that brought her to acknowledge the call hidden since she was born again. She was never more serious in her life and focused that formidable determination on GOING. The singular anointing resting on her and a genuine missions call was recognized by church officials and Mary and C. P. Williams, Directors of Apostolic College in Tulsa, Oklahoma, where she enrolled in 1946.

There is a glimpse of Gladys hunched over the steering wheel of a flatbed Model T, hair bound in a bandana, suitcases and necessary paraphernalia tied down, on an evangelistic sweep that touched several churches. She was not oblivious of the chagrin and discomfort of 17-year-old daughter Carmen and a dear friend, but she moved with purpose, God's will must be done, whatever the cost.

Now, facing inevitable sacrifice she marvelled over God's direction. Sometime before there had been contact and instant affinity with Georgia

Regenhardt, missionary in charge of Maheh Mission in Liberia, West Africa. They fondly called each other Robbie and Reggie. She was delighted by the Mission Board's decision that she should go to Maheh to assist Reggie.

Chapter 2

WHERE ARE YOU?

The bustle and flurry of leaving climaxed at Jackson, Tennessee, train station the 31st of July 1947. Loving family and friends waved, 'Goodbye' until the train was out of sight.

"I'm on my way to Africa alone, leaving all to follow Jesus—reasonable service considering all He has given me. I don't understand my divided heart—I have sweet peace, yet a part of me aches over leaving my babies for three years or more. I rejoice to go, yet, cannot shake off uneasiness about the trip and my future. God's Word must be my anchor now," Gladys suddenly realized.

She read the account of Israel's miraculous passage through the Red Sea for encouragement, then II Timothy 2:3 *". . . endure hardness as a good soldier"* for a reprimand to weakness of the flesh. Eventually she slept.

The rapidly changing view from her window the next day was sometimes lovely—miles of Blue Ridge Mountains—and often interesting—a huge blimp in the sky over Washington, D. C.

New York City's massive impact was softened by Brother Rubin, one of the pastors in the City, meeting her. They tried unsuccessfully to reach the office where she could get the necessary yellow fever innoculation before it closed. She was amazed at subway travel—over and under water.

Three letters from Georgia were waiting for her.

"Maheh Mission
June 26, 1947

"Dear Sister Robbie,

God bless you! For more than a month we've all been praying, "God bless Sister Robinson on her way." I guess we can continue a little longer!

God has given me grace for the thing I said I couldn't do—take care of the people of two missions alone. No, not alone, for Jesus has been my comfort, my help and my shield. More than anything I need someone to counsel with. Every day new problems arise—never know what a day will bring. I'm glad God knows!

Yes, my dear, I know it takes plenty of God's grace to leave your Darlings. My girls love me so much, it wasn't easy to say 'Goodbye' but they have companions to comfort them. But, oh, my boy, how he hated to see me leave! It was hard, but Jesus was so sweetly near. Bless your heart, God will not let us down. We'll share our joys and sorrows, and someday lay sheaves from Africa at our Savior's feet. Won't we?

I would love to meet you, but looks impossible. Sister Holmes is waiting for you at Monrovia, she's very sweet. Don't fear the rains, I'll send a big umbrella and rubber boots, and with the hammock you'll make it.

Hurry now!

Love, Reggie"

"Maheh Mission
July 2, 1947

"My Dear Sister Robbie,

Why, oh, why, don't you come? I have been sending mission boys every week hoping to get a radiogram about your arrival.

But, Jesus is making the waiting easier by pouring out His Spirit in our midst. Four were filled with the Holy Ghost last week. Let us pray earnestly that God will be pleased to give us a mighty, glorious, sweeping revival!

Don't forget to send a cable to the Schaumburgs at the Assemblies of God Mission Home in Monrovia. It's over 40 miles from Roberts Field where you will land to Monrovia, so I've arranged for them to meet you. Sister Holmes may be able to wait for you—otherwise I'll send some dependable mission boys to help you.

God bless you and give you a safe and speedy journey to us.

Your own
Sister Reggie"

"Monrovia
July 17, 1947

"Dear Sister Robbie,

Oh, where are you? I've been looking for you

since the first of June. I wanted so much to meet you here.

I left the children in the teachers' care and came on as my checks were delayed and had to be cashed. But I can neither stay longer nor come back later. I'm hoping Sister Holmes will still be here, but, I'll send a boy every week until you come.

God bless you 'plenty'.

Do hurry!

Sister Reggie"

"Reggie, if you only knew how much I want to hurry! But I am faced with customary 15-day delay in travel after the yellow fever innoculation, besides uncertain booking. Be patient, O my soul!"

The Rubins took Gladys sightseeing Saturday ending the tour at LaGuardia Airfield. She didn't know planes were made so large, an overseas Clipper made her want to board at once for Africa. Sunday, she was beset by loneliness for her babies and thought longingly of the Camp Meeting where so many she loved were gathered to worship. But, the day ended brightly with a powerful message on "The Greatness of God" by Andrew Urshan, the grand old man of Pentecost, at his church on 92nd Street.

Monday brought good news, along with the yellow fever shot she learned the usual fifteen-day delay before traveling was no longer required. She called Brother Elmo Hopkins, banker, travel agent and friend of missionaries in Indianapolis, and announced she was ready to go! He told her reservations were made for August the 18th on Pan Am connecting with Air France in Dakar and he was sending her passport, visa and ticket. She went to the Pan Am office to see if an earlier flight was available and made shipping arrangements for her trunks on a boat leaving August the 8th. Freddie, eighteen-year-old son of the hospitable Rubin family, took her to the places she needed to go with a side trip to Staten Island and the Statue of Liberty.

Wednesday, August 6th was overshadowed by two big IFs—IF there was a cancellation on the flight the next day, and IF her ticket and passport came in time, she might be able to leave earlier. In the late afternoon Pan Am phoned flight confirmation leaving 6:00 A.M. August 7th and still later, in God's exquisite timing the ticket, visa and passport arrived!

Gladys phoned Sister Gurley in Corinth to let her daughters know the time of departure and wrote them a final letter.

"Now, listen Girls!

Whenever anything goes wrong I expect you to let me know so I can pray with you. I'll do the same, then we won't be imagining something that may not exist.

The Rubins have prayed with me and we feel it is God's time, however I'm especially anxious that prayers will be going up for the next few days. There may be a long layover in Dakar—can't get confirmed reservations on to Liberia. Don't expect a letter too soon—there's only two planes a week. Dearest Marie and Carmen! Be good servants of the Lord, then my home-

coming will be happy. Stay close to God, then if I need prayer He will show you instantly.

Love and Kisses
Mother"

She thought of Reggie's letters, "Where am I? Oh, Reggie, I'm still in New York City, but, God willing, I'll soon be on my way!"

Chapter 3
TEDIOUS TREK

August 7th—main thing moving at 6:00 A.M. was rain pouring down in great sheets. Departure postponed until 6:00 P.M. She prayed for "waiting" grace in the long day, then another seven and a half hours delay was announced—departure time 1:30 A.M.

Two o'clock A.M., August 8th, take-off at last! She reminded the Lord of His promise, "I will uphold thee."

Goodbye, America!

"Father, I leave my babies in Your care. Help me gather jewels from the jungles for You."

The plane called "the Invincible" was monstrous to her. Its occasional drops and rises made her dizzy and encouraged renewal of her trust in God. She wryly admitted in the beginning of the flight, "I may be closer to God up here but my peace is more settled when I don't look down."

There were only thirteen passengers, most of them slept, but one couldn't for tears kept falling. Every thought of her children brought a fresh shower until the Spirit comforted her with words from the Psalms:

"Weeping may endure for a night, but joy cometh in the morning." Psa. 30:5b

Soon there was bright blue sky overhead and she looked down on white clouds giving the amazing impression of vast barren plains covered with snow-drifts. She could not help but thrill with the majesty of God revealed in His creation.

When the view grew sombre with dark storm clouds and the plane rocked in the pressure, she sang softly, "Jesus Saviour pilot me."

The first stop was on Azores Island where the passengers had dinner under a big umbrella at Hotel Nastra. Next stop Lisbon, Portugal, beautiful from the air, and quaint on the ground. She bought two bunches of flowers to send home—later discovered they were covered almonds. Leaving Lisbon, the plane was full. A French boy sat by her and they struggled to communicate without understanding each other's language.

Over the Sahara Desert heat was oppressive in the plane. She wilted looking down on sand, sand, sand, with only an occasional touch of green—small tree or shrub.

Dakar! The plane landed at twelve noon Senegal time and Gladys touched Africa for the first time. In the more leisurely travel of those days, she made friends on board. Many wished her well, a young man said, "Let them have it!" One lady asked her to please let her know or she would be wondering the rest of her life how she made it on to Liberia. She watched them leave and felt surprisingly alone.

After customary immigration, customs and police

formalities, she found a room with meals for $7.00 a day thankfully shared with some American ladies, part of a missionary group of the United Brethren enroute to Freetown, Sierra Leone. They had been waiting four days, Gladys joined them hoping for reservations soon on Air France. They were told no bookings available until October though planes went out three times a week.

From her window she saw sand, flowering shrubs and a few gnarled, ancient trees. Some of the men wore short pants, most dressed in loose kimono-type robes. The women appeared to wear several layers of those voluminous garments, nearly always with matching scarves intricately tied into turbans. It was not unusual for a group of women to stop in the road, set down the high stacked loads from their heads, change robes, replace their burdens and journey on. Small nude boys played across the road. The natives were interesting, but their hygiene habits most embarrassing!

She arranged paper napkins to cover the grimy dresser top in the room, washed a few things in the wash basin and felt refreshed after a shower. She examined the sheets on the bed longing to lie down and rest, but they were filthy.

A group of the missionaries walked to the seashore after supper to watch the large white-crested waves roll in. Looking over the sea to the sunset from the point on the African continent nearest America, she felt so far from her beloved family, but realized she dare not dwell on such thoughts. "I've committed them to Jesus," she whispered to the soft evening air,

"I must leave them in His hands. Oh, but I'm glad He understands a mother's love and her tears of longing."

Eight thirty P.M., still no clean sheets, she decided to ask. The manager took some from a vacant bed in the men's room, said they were unused and all that was available. They looked and smelled dirty, but she sprinkled them liberally with talcum powder, boiled water in an old percolator to brush her teeth and went to bed with a prayer. The roar of the ocean, only two blocks distant, was too loud for a lullaby but exhaustion brought sleep.

Sunday morning as she made her bed, a boy came in.

"Do you want boiled water?"

"Yes, please."

He left, later returned with another boy and without water.

"Hot water?"

"Yes, please." She gave each of them a stick of gum.

"Do you want coffee?"

"No thanks."

"Do you want juice?"

"No, I'll come down for breakfast."

The hot water finally came and iced pineapple juice as well.

She saw the first African village in the afternoon, with huts made of straw or matting of some kind, watched the women carrying water on their heads and longed to tell them about Jesus, but they couldn't understand her.

She met her first lion and leopard outside the town, and stood her ground, they stood theirs—in a cage, of course!

Sunday night listening to the furious pounding of the waves she thought, "My great God commands them and they obey Him. He walks on them as on a carpet. He's my Father and able to keep my children I've committed to His care!" It seemed every day there had to be a renewal of that commitment to keep her heart at ease.

When she went to the American Consulate Monday in a one-horse sort of taxi, the impressive American flag waving outside brought tears to her eyes. Air France gave her good news—reservations to Roberts Field for Thursday, August 14th, 5:30 A.M. Her friends learned with disappointment the Freetown Airport was flooded, so more delay for them.

The cable Reggie advised her to send cost $9.00, she hesitated but wisdom insisted so it was sent.

She was annoyed by swarms of mangy dogs around the hotel. A porter said, "They don't understand English, yell "allez!" at them, that is the French equivalent of "Get out."

She used the new word vigorously but they didn't always "allez!"

Looking, shopping and taking pictures were spaced to help pass the waiting time. She asked a tall young man if he was a Christian. He answered, "No, Mohamedan."

She tried in vain to tell him of her mission and the One Who sent her. She saw the Moslems worshipping repeatedly, kneeling toward Mecca, their holy city, and was told there are no Protestant churches in Dakar. But she kept on trying. A pleasant young man followed them along the street, she turned, "Do you know Jesus?"

"No, me don't know Him, me know nutting."

"He died on the cross to save you from sin." He looked puzzled.

"Don't know Him, me know nutting."

"I'm going to tell others," she thought, "but here are so many fine, friendly young men. When will someone come to bring them the whole Gospel?"

Departure day, the Junker left nearly on time with twelve passengers, one of them an American. She could neither talk nor be talked to with any satisfaction. Sometimes they seemed to hang in the air only two hundred feet above rivers, jungles and swamps. Every detail was plainly seen of mud huts and the people standing outside. Low cloud clusters buffed and tossed the small plane. Looking for diversion from the anxieties of the hazardous journey, she remembered the letters received in New York City from many wishing her Godspeed. She reread them and concluded every writer had been anointed of God.

She thought the one stop between Dakar and Roberts Field at Konaky was an emergency landing. The little gravel-sprinkled runway looked like anything but a landing field.

How good Roberts Field looked after seven torturous hours getting there! Paved runways and everyone speaking English took the sting out of not being met. She felt like she had been suspended by a thread for hours dangling in midair. There were no tears for the departure of Air France; she wished that both Reggie and her family could know that she had arrived. Customs officers were kind and soon she sat on a bench alone in front of the airport suronded by her luggage—waiting and wondering with a strange let-down feeling.

Two thirty P.M., Reverend Congo came for her in the A. G. Mission truck. They made several stops on the way to Monrovia. He showed her a deserted army chapel surrounded by palm trees near the airport.

"It would make a beautiful church—but, no funds available," he lamented.

At Trader Horn's place she saw wild animals collected to send to California. While waiting she walked close to the river, watched the Firestone boat go by, and heard something unseen crawl through the grass as she returned to the truck.

Every tree, flower and bird was different to those seen before, but the songs of strange birds were pleasant. The women carried babies on their back tied with a piece of cloth, most of them wore only skirts. Some men and women had on long robes and quite a few were in Western dress. She wanted to take pictures, but, sudden tropical rain sent her scurrying to the shelter of the truck's cab. She was given her first African banana and pronounced it delicious.

They reached the Schaumburgs at 5:00 P.M. in time for a good American supper. There she learned how precisely she was led. The Schaumburgs were away for three weeks, returned home the night before her cable came. The traveling delays saved her being stranded in Monrovia!

Friday, August 15th, while they were wondering how to get word to Reggie, two boys from Maheh Mission came, Kenny (about twenty) and John (about sixteen). Kenny was sick, but, fleetfooted John started back at once with the exciting news, "Mother' Robinson has arrived!"

While waiting for helpers for the trip Mother Robinson got acquainted with the sights, sounds, smells and customs of Monrovia. She reported to Police Headquarters and was fingerprinted, registered at the Immigration office, the Department of Interior, and the American Consulate.

A teacher from the mission on sick leave came to see her and told her the new teacher would go with her to the mission.

Rain! Rain! Rain!

She sent a cable to Marie and bought a white cork-lined helmet for six dollars. There was a big funeral in town, since there are no embalming facilities, the dead must be buried right away. Church bells tolled as four men carried the casket on their heads. A band played all the way to the cemetery and back, same tune over and over, sounded like the first four lines of "Little Brown Jug." A group of mourners dressed in black followed the band.

The Schaumburgs were very kind to her but faced an urgent problem. Their two-year-old son had a serious kidney disease, the doctor told them they must take him back to the States immediately and there was no one to take their place.

Bedtime, the separation-from-her-family heartache

came to haunt her again. She wrestled through with Scripture, ". . . my grace is sufficient for thee," and rationalized, "After all, this life is only a vapor that soon vanishes—it shouldn't matter so much. If we can all just make it inside the gate, we'll be together forever."

She wrote her children:

"Don't let up on prayer for me. I'd hate to be in Africa without Divine protection. But with THAT, it's alright.

"I don't have much to write now, but I'll send a letter back with my first chance. You'll have to wait until I get to the mission, then I can tell you about trekking through the jungles; how many leopards I killed and how many boa constrictors I crushed under my heel on the way out.

"I received my first letter, this lady thought I have been here for some time.

"Write soon.

"Much Love
Mother"

The plans were to go up the river about two hours on a boat to Waterside, then walk to Arlington by dark and spend the night in the home of an elderly African lady who kept travellers. The carriers would meet her there and take her on to Maheh.

While she packed again on Monday, she hummed an old song:

"Here I'm bothered with packing
each time that I move
And I carry a load in each hand,

But I'll not need one thing
That I've used in this world
When I move to that heavenly land."

Eight o'clock p.m.that night the mission boys Jason and Alfred arrived. They had walked since 11:00 a.m. Sunday and all night. They took a truck at White Plains, but it stalled and they were delayed most of the day on the road. They left their rice with the carriers at Waterside, so had nothing to eat. She gave them part of her rations and bought them some rice. Alfred was barefooted and hurt his toe on the way, but they didn't pause. Jason explained, "We hurry to get you!"

They brought a letter from Reggie:

"Excitement is running high here. I dreamed Friday night you came and I asked 'Robbie, is it really you?' The very next day John dashed in calling, 'Mother Regenhardt, Mother Robinson has come!' The children came running as the news spread. John was questioned and his eyes rolled in excitement as he told the good news.

I can hardly wait till you reach Maheh.

Love
Reggie"

The river boat was due to leave at 2:00 p.m. Gladys bought everything on the list that Georgia sent and besides fifty pounds of flour at $7.40 for a special treat. Alfred got lost in town, she sent Jason to find him. Alfred returned, so Kenny went to hunt for Jason. The two missing boys and the teacher, with her baby tied on her back, came running, almost out of breath. The boat left at 2:30 with seventy five people wedged on board with their bundles, crates and suitcases. The rain that started in the morning slacked at times, but continued all day.

Gladys watched the banks through falling rain; swamps, palms, banana trees and native huts, some with metal roofs. The teacher ate a belated lunch of bread and canned milk.

The river that seemed narrow at first widened. Jason pointed out landmarks as they passed, New Jersey, Louisiana and Virginia. High water prevented their landing at Virginia as planned. They sailed by a long stretch thick with houses surrounded by fields of cane from which brown sugar and rum is made.

They reached Waterside at 4:00 p.m. Young men from the Mission and carriers rushed out to meet the boat. Each one shook her hand and said shyly, "Hello Ma!" Much time was spent preparing hammocks for Gladys and the teacher and sorting the loads. Some of the teacher's luggage and the groceries were set aside to wait for another trip—not enough carriers.

Gladys considered the slippery mud of the trail and tried the boots sent by Georgia. They were too flat, so she put on her oxfords and the motley cavalcade moved slowly down the path. The mission boys tried to help her up a slick bank and Jason fell flat. She dug in her heels and managed to stay upright—a feat that brightened the day with spontaneous laughter. She and the teacher walked for nearly an hour slipping and sliding in the mud before getting in the hammocks. She asked,

"Am I heavy?"

"Huh!"

"Am I as heavy as Mother Regenhardt?"

"No Ma'am."

She thought mischieveously, "I'll remember to tell Reggie that!"

The load the men carried seemed so cruel. One struggled along with her footlocker on his head—she knew how heavy it was! The teacher's two older children were tied to the backs of men who carried boxes on their heads, others had suitcases and bundles. The two front hammock carriers lifted the hammock high above their heads down steep hills, the two carrying the back did the same uphill. She prayed for God to give them strength and was convinced He did for they trotted down the path making a game of the journey.

"Should we try to reach Suehn tonight?"

Jason and the carriers discussed the possibility. Suehn was a Baptist mission where Christianity was translated into hospitality and helping hands. It would have been a comfortable place to stay. However, daylight decided for them by making a wet, speedy exit as they neared Arlington. Gladys approached the crush of humanity on the front porch of Arlington with apprehensions. Dim, flickering lanterns and the strident babble of voices emphasized her uneasiness. Jason said,

"Wait here while I find out if there's place for us to sleep."

She felt better when five little girls detached

themselves from the crowd and greeted her. They talked to her a few minutes, then, lady-like, excused themselves. Jason returned,

"You can share a room with the teacher and some women. The rest of us will sleep in a room without beds on the third floor."

In her room she found a teacher and group of girls from the Holmes' mission at Zordee waiting for carriers. The girls she met on the porch were part of them. She thought

"Now I know why they were so mannerly." In her heart she gave thanks,

> *"How marvelous are your ways, Dear Lord! You have sweetened an unpalatable situation by putting me with your children. I don't know why I wondered before dark if you were still leading me—you always do! Thank you, Jesus."*

Pleasant time together encouraged plans for more fellowship on the trail. Distance was never figured in miles, but rather in walking time. Since Zordee was only three hours from Maheh, they hoped to walk together for about seven hours the next day.

Disappointment! Zordee carriers didn't come in time. Although the lady who owned the home at Arlington did not charge for lodging, Gladys gave her a dollar, and they were off, Jason leading his group on the trail early.

Until 9:00 a.m. they were on an old road bed. In spite of the fearful creek-crossing on a big log, she decided, "This isn't too bad." Then the path became progressively rougher. Vines and tree limbs intertwined overhead in thick gloom. Coarse saw grass closed in almost head high. She was carried over two streams, one river was negotiated with a raft. They crossed the Poe River by turns in a canoe, its waters swift from heavy rains. When she was walking she continually watched for worms similar to centipedes—many of them were a foot long. She told the teacher,

"If one of those things fall on me, I'll be across the stream before they have time to carry me over!"

They stopped briefly at a village. An old man laying on a mat before the fire got up and came to greet her. Topless women in long skirts pounded rice in large vessels, most of them smiled. The men said, "Good morning, Ma!"

Trudge on and on, hour after hour. She thought,

"Surely it can't get worse than this." The jungle proved her wrong. Permeating odor of decaying vegetation hovered over a trail winding steeply up grade. Footing was precarious through slick patches of clay, protruding roots and tricky holes. They moved in a murky tunnel where sinuous vines and twisted branches rampantly choked each other in the density. Ferns, four and five feet tall, crammed in odd nooks unfurled their delicate leaves. The weird atmosphere was emphasized by trees with roots sprouting three or four feet high on the trunk, going to the ground like flying buttresses. Creeping under the roots was sometimes the best way through.

The travelers were strung out along the narrow path for a mile or so. When bone weary from walking she submitted to the jolting of the hammock for awhile. A prickle of fear caught her breath on a walking turn—something black and white moving on the path ahead! Breathe again, Gladys, it's only a goat.

The next obstacle was a large pile of brush, sticky to crawl over. A wild call that sounded like insane laughter sent another chill down her spine. The guide noticed her alarm and explained, "That's a big bird."

A huge tree had fallen across the path, lodged against another tree and accumulated an enormous heap of debris. This they squirmed under, one by one. She couldn't help but question,

"Lord, are you leading me? Can there be enough people in a place like this to merit such distance, expense and effort to bring them the Gospel?"

There was no direct answer, however, courage and strength to keep moving did not falter. Steady rain either pelted them or dribbled through leaves on them for most of the day. She often wished it would stop, though when it did, the scorching sun let them walk in hot steam. The cool rain was welcome when it came again.

Her hammock showed signs of falling apart causing a stop for repairs, then she traded hammocks with the lighter teacher and they jogged on. The carriers' fatigue was evident, so she walked as much as possible. Since her feet had been wet all day, there was no need to avoid puddles—splatter on through! Weariness slowed the jogging and trotting but the carriers continued to sing. They made up songs as they went, one sang a line and the others repeated it with variations. She was sure they could be heard for a mile or more.

She was carried across the third stream with rising appreciation for the rivers that had makeshift bridges of logs, vines and bamboo. Her opinion had changed from the beginning of the trek based on a better understanding of the dangerous African crocodile.

"We're an hour and a half from the Mission!" Jason announced.

Suddenly, Gladys realized how anxious she was for the end of the journey. She had travelled for twenty days by train, plane, truck, riverboat, canoe, raft, hammock and foot. As they went through the next village clearing she considered her muddy hose and shoes in the fading light and thought wistfully it would be nice to clean up before reaching the mission.

The boys bought bush-hog meat in the following village. The trail beyond it led through dense jungle, home of many monkeys, including the rare long-maned Lion monkey. She was watching monkey antics when the carriers yelled, "Look out!"

Instantly, her legs felt as though they were on fire. She had walked into the wide, black path of a column of marching Driver Ants. She stomped her feet while everyone near helped knock the fierce little creatures off her legs. They plodded on as darkness settled around them, Jason's flashlight leading the sodden parade.

"Fifteen minutes to the Mission!" he called. Gladys felt excitement rise in spite of fatigue. They approached a long narrow bridge over a brimming turbulent river. Jason offered a helping hand, but by this time she was accustomed to African bridges. She was confident they would support her weight however rickety they looked and thought she was fully able to walk across without assistance. Besides, they were so near the Mission everyone wanted to hurry. Jason ahead, Kenny behind her and two carriers with the empty hammock reached the middle section when there was a sudden, loud crash and all five of them were floundering in agitated water.

Jason yelled as they fell, then shock brought stupefying silence. Gladys grabbed her purse, the $6 helmet she tried to protect from rain for two days floated near and she rescued it. She thought of African snakes and shivered as Jason's metal lunch kit sailed by. Just as she wondered where he was, he called excitedly behind her.

"Oh, Mother Robinson! Are you all right?"

"Yes, Jason, I'm O.K. Let's be calm and do something practical. How about getting us out of the river?"

She tried to move toward the bank, but the broken bridge was in the way. Somehow Jason pulled her over the wreckage and together they got Kenny out. The valise he carried floated until retrieved. Kenny's hip was bruised, but when he realized the towel was missing that he used for padding on his head under the valise, he dived back in to look for it. While the carriers and hammock were being fished out, the humor of the situation hit Gladys and she laughed until she remembered Kenny's injury and noticed she laughed alone. There may have been a tinge of hysteria in her mirth.

Jason felt the urgency of delivering his charge to the mission so he rushed her away. While she stumbled in the darkness trying to follow his flashlight, she wondered how the rest of the group would cross the river.

The last mile would never be forgotten. She thought longingly of a bath and clean, dry clothes while her feet cautiously felt for solid places to step. It had to be done quickly for Jason was going faster, almost running. The two half-drowned carriers straggled along behind them.

"There it is!" exclaimed Jason. She looked up through the rain to where a small light glimmered from the crest of the hill and thanked God that her goal was in sight. Drenched and dripping with torn hose, sand-filled shoes, muddy dress, smeared helmet and wet hair falling down Gladys came nearer the circle of light where the children waited for her under lanterns.

Chapter 4

MOTHER ROBINSON HAS ARRIVED!

The children's faded, spotless clothes looked white in the dim light. When they realized she was near, their voices lifted in fervent song.

"We're marching to Zion.
Beautiful, beautiful Zion.
We're marching upward to Zion
The beautiful City of God."

Over and over, the lovely words rang out. Down the trail she questioned, "Is the Lord still leading me?" There was no answer then, it came now, in the children's song. "Yes, yes, yes!" Tears mingled with rain on her face as she rushed toward them speaking in tongues and praising Jesus. She saw their shining black faces through tears and tried to hug all fifty-two of them at once. She picked up a wee one and together they 'marched' on to the mission to meet Mother Regenhardt.

The two friends embraced with happy tears. Gladys glanced around. The immaculate mission house looked inviting with linoleum covered floors, white sheets and mosquito nets on the beds. After the longed-for hot bath and tasty chicken with palm butter supper, the children were ushered reluctantly to their sleeping quarters. She tiptoed to the babies' room to admire the dusky cherubs in repose; their ages ranged from four to sixteen months.

Delicious chatter came before sleep. Georgia gave a summary of mission activities and plans. Gladys relayed many messages and recounted her trip. They talked until exhaustion put out the light at 1:00 a.m.

By daylight Gladys was up and out on a tour of the mission, anxious to see her surroundings. The mission complex was large and beautifully laid out. Beajah mission had recently combined with Maheh because of insufficient workers and funds, giving Georgia a double load. Their charges at Maheh now, were four babies, fifty-two children assorted ages and seven grown young men, the hope for future evangelism.

Maheh had smooth lawns, close-cropped by mission boys plying grass hooks, neat scraped paths and clean orchards. Pineapple plants marched in orderly rows next to lime, papaya, grapefruit and banana trees. Many buildings were constructed of mud and thatch; boys' quarters, girls' quarters bath-house, workshed, washhouse, storage house, separate kitchens for boys and girls, workmen's quarters and chicken house. The combined chapel and school building and two residences had metal roofs. Mats woven of bamboo made partitions and ceilings. Until the Haneys returned from furlough, they were living temporarily in their house with the advantage of wood floors over mud ones in the other dwelling.

Gladys heard her first buy-sell "palaver" that morning. Men from the village came with handmade cloth to sell. Georgia wanted the cloth to send home and bargained for it like a true African.

While they ate dinner, Rachel (an older girl on the mission) came in wringing her hands, tears streaming, gasping and choking with protruded tongue.

"Bad case of asthma," thought Gladys and waited for Georgia to take appropriate action, but all she said was,

"I see you've done it again."

"Uh huh," came the teary reply. Georgia explained,

"They dearly love peppers. I gave them a can of hot ones to last several days, and they've put every one in their chop at one time."

She gave her a greasy potato to cool the burning and she left still blinking tears and uncomfortable. The ladies could not help but smile in spite of the girl's misery.

In the afternoon Georgia showed her the crude runway nearing completion. They called it the "airport"—ambitious exaggeration. They anticipated the blessing when Brother Haney would return with a plane that could simplify their acute transport problems.

"You know, Reggie," said Gladys, "These are our brothers in Christ and I feel for them with aching heads from the heavy loads they carry and torn feet from the snags of the trail. Oh! a plane will help so much."

Everyone gathered for services at 6:30 p.m. The singing rang out as Kenny led choruses. Some shouted and rejoiced, a few fell slain under the power. Two unsaved boys felt convicted and asked forgiveness for mocking. The testimonies were earnest and sincere. They expressed gratitude for the missionaries who brought them the light and concern for their families still living in the darkness of sin. Jack wept and said he wanted to go to other villages to witness when the rains let up.

When the bustle of the day was done, the two friends relived the past few days. Some events, not comical at the time were hilarious viewed in relaxed retrospect, memories of the collapsed bridge, the way Gladys looked on arrival and Rachel and her peppers triggered school-girl giggles. They laughed until both of them were wiping away tears. Mission work is often grim—it must be a merciful God who sends some light-hearted moments for balance.

6:00 a.m. the horn blew a call to prayer. The boys went to the chapel with Georgia while the girls met with Gladys in the big kitchen. They prayed together for the daily needs, for each other, for revival, and for friends and family. They sang choruses and she talked to them about Jesus.

The boys came to Georgia for job assignments, she was busy every moment. Gladys moved softly charting the adjustment course and finding her place in the daily program. The first necessity was honing her ears to "hear" the children. She recalled when on the trail, Jason was the only one she could really understand. Though they all spoke English, it was quaint, Liberian English with idioms and terminology strange to her American ears. When they said, "Ah-skuce" they meant "Excuse me," "I met it" meant "I found it," "Lay down" meant "go to bed."

Gladys found many pineapple sprouts and decided to plant them near the house they would live in on the Haneys return. Jack was in charge of 'plantation pineapple,' he drafted a group of helpers and they went to gather the young plants. Gladys reached for one, gave a wild scream and ran over Jack trying to get away. She said "ah-skuce" and pointed a trembling finger to the snake coiled around the sprout she had thought to pull. A small boy with the official title of "snake killer" took over. He didn't kill the poisonous caesava snake who escaped to his hole in the commotion, however, she was assured he would be afraid to come out, so enough pineapples were planted for daily use and to can.

Georgia arranged a teaching session for the young men with a call to preach. Just as they came together in the chapel, all eyes suddenly focused on the rafters where a large snake lay. One of the boys poked it with a pole, it swung out striking, and the missionaries edged toward the door. The snake was soon knocked down and permanently out. When the battle was over, the service continued with blessing and ended with renewed consecration.

Gladys 'adopted' four-months-old Ruth, adding Mary to her name in honor of her friend, Mary Williams. The older girls whose responsibility was to care for the smaller girls and babies did not like to tend spoilt Ruthie. They said,

"She humbugs us too much!"

Sunday School Children

The older boys looked after the younger ones in the 'family' climate the missionaries endeavored to build.

Her first Sunday on the mission seventy-five came for Sunday school. Sick women from the village came asking medicine. Gladys invited them to attend the evening service and meet the physician. The town chief came with them. She preached on "Saving and Healing Power" with Jason interpreting into the local vernacular. Three women responded; she dealt with each of them personally about leaving sin and serving Jesus, with Jason's help. They prayed long together before they left rejoicing. One of the women held her hand and said,

"We know you have something we don't have or you wouldn't have left your people and come so far to tell us about God's power. We want to learn to trust Jesus as you do."

The children often expressed their love and longing for the return of those who in times past worked at Beajah and Maheh missions. Kenny testified,

"I pray the Lord will cause them to 'study about us' until they have to come back to Liberia."

August 30th, Red Letter Day! Jack and Kenny returned at 8:00 p.m. with the yield of post office Box 44. Georgia had a stack of mail and Gladys rejoiced over five letters, two of them the first news from her family since she arrived at Maheh.

When the Pettys went on furlough (just before she came) Georgia agreed to buy the American food they had left over for $390.00—a most reasonable price for the quantity of groceries. In the everyday business of living Gladys assumed half of this debt which they paid off in installments. She bought half interest in the chickens and both ladies were thankful for two Coleman lanterns they bought from an independent missionary family leaving for the states. The kerosene lamps previously used did not shed enough light in the chapel to locate possible worms, spiders, scorpions or snakes. Gladys still shivered remembering the huge, woolly black worm the boys dispatched just before it got to her in that first service.

There was much to appreciate; large oranges at 16 cents a dozen for refreshing juice, and bananas from the village for 15 cents a stalk when none were ripe on the Mission. The Pentecostal Bible Institute in Tupelo, Mississippi, blessed Georgia regularly with packages of canned preserves and candy. Gladys looked forward to her family and friends remembering her with packages so she would have something to share.

She learned the burning power of tropical sunshine and what a good investment the $6 helmet was. She found it unwise to neglect a cut or a pimple, for the smallest scratch festered rapidly, and discovered with amazement that even Gladys needed extra rest to handle tropical fatigue. She prayed,

"Dear Lord, in your will, I'm in Liberia at last! Oh, make me a blessing in your name!"

Chapter 5

LEARNING

One morning she checked the kitchen where mission girls Gladys and Dorcas were preparing breakfast. Four year old Moses stood before the hearth, his eyes fixed expectantly on the ashes.

"Run along, Moses, the girls are busy here." Turning, he grabbed something out of the ashes.

"May I see?" she asked. It was a big fat grasshopper complete with eyes, legs and insides nicely roasted.

"Wouldn't you like to give this delicacy to Mother Regenhardt for her breakfast?" she suggested. His reluctance was evident but he handed it over.

"Thank you very much, Moses," she said kindly. A few minutes later loud wails came from under the house where Moses grieved over his lost grasshopper. They called him in and Georgia returned his treasure.

"I've one request," said Gladys. "Just get out of sight before you take a bite."

The gun sent Georgia by a friend was in Monrovia. She planned to go get it and bring home Gladys' trunks that had arrived. Jason, Willie and Gladys walked to Maheh village in the evening looking for hammock men for the trip. They passed a hut where a woman, clothed only in a loin cloth sat on the ground screaming. Someone said the baby was dying. Gladys looked inside. Seven or eight women were gathered around the desperately sick infant. They splashed it with cold water until it shivered, then with water hot enough to steam—it cried feebly. She tried to comfort the mother, too distraught with grief to understand her words. The old grandmother was frantic, she thought the witch doctor was going to eat the baby. The village was very dark except for the flickering dim light of a few kerosene filled bottles with a wick. The spiritual darkness and ignorance was even more oppressive. The hammock men thought the weather was too bad to travel. Gladys trudged back with a heavy heart. When would God's light illumine the age-old darkness?

Two girls came unexpectedly from Monrovia with a letter from the Schaumburgs.

Dear Georgia and Gladys,

We are leaving with our sick baby. Nancy Ann and Victoria have no place to go. They are Christians and willing workers, we can't turn them out on the streets. Please let them stay at the mission with you—we'll send support for them.

Gladys, we will mail the Iguana skin billfolds and purses you bought for your children's Christmas gifts when we get to the States.

Thanks!

They couldn't refuse the girls who proved to be assets. Nancy Ann was especially competent with the small children and babies, kept them happy and shining clean.

Another baby died in the village. They heard the wails of mourning all night long. The father was reproachful,

"You could have saved my baby," he said. However, the Mission Board decreed, "No more children to be taken in the mission." They understood all the logical reasons for this, but still, it was hard to turn them away to die.

Sister Jiles, Pentecostal missionary from five days' walk farther back in the interior came by. Her plea for help at the mission she manned alone touched the heart of Gladys—if only there were more workers!

Glorious services were a frequent bonus. In one, three mission girls and the new teacher received the Holy Ghost. Many of the village folk sought God, several workers were filled with the Spirit. Some of the young people prayed with the seekers while others beat tambourines and sang. When they swung out on, "I'll be somewhere working for my Lord," Gladys got her share of the blessing, she didn't know they knew the song and it was one of her favorites from the time she was saved. She always thought of Africa when she sang it, now she heard it in Liberia!

A baptismal service was planned in the Maheh river which winds on two sides of the mission, but, the river swollen by rains came out for the occasion. Twenty five candidates were baptized on the lawn several yards from the river's normal banks. The next day the waters had receded and grass on the site glistened in the sun.

Azmona, one of the workmen gave her a nature-study lesson. He showed her what appeared to be a sand rock, then broke it open—inside was a Queen bug-a-bug (termite). Her head was about the size of a wasp, and her body looked like a very large grub worm. Several bug-a-bugs were tending her, they looked like large ants with wings. He explained,

"If she is buried there will soon be a bug-a-bug hill four or five feet high."

She often rested in a hammock hung in the outdoor kitchen. This was a separate square building behind the house with dried palm leaf thatch. The mud floor had a foot high wall of mud all around with woven wire extending to the ceiling made of woven mats. Palm branches were woven through the wire to keep out sun and glare. Georgia explained,

"When the hot, dry weather comes, this will be our living room."

The hot, dry weather was yet to come, for in her first three weeks on the mission there was only one day of sunshine! The river had overflowed again and washed away the bridge to the boys' dormitory. Since they had to swim back and forth, morning and night and this was dangerous after dark, the Bible studies were discontinued for a while.

The boys killed a baby boa constrictor four feet long in the garden. The ladies wished they knew where its papa and mama were hiding!

Nancy Ann, Gladys, Dorcas, Victoria and Rebecca asked permission to go to the village for a visit to

Dorcas' mother who was recently baptized. Gladys sent an old dress for her remembering that she had nothing but a small cloth wrapped around her hips. Her gratitude was overwhelming. How she longed for more to give!

Gladys woke up one morning hungry for meat and that day a strange man brought them venison—roast and dressing for supper was a welcome treat. She marvelled that God had supplied her desire so quickly.

September the 4th and the 20th, Box 44 produced letters from home, the biggest news—she was now Grandma! Allan and his wife Verla had a baby girl named Rita Joy. When would she ever be privileged to see and hold that little darling?

Kenny and Jack were delayed at Monrovia because of high water, but brought two of her trunks when they came, a missionary friend cleared them through customs. The third trunk waited at Waterside until Jason went for it. The kerosene refrigerator her friends bought for Georgia was at Millsboro and would probably have to wait there until the dry season.

Gladys felt ill Sunday, September 28th and went back to bed after a sweet service with a fine message by Georgia. She insisted on preaching as planned that night. Her message was, "Pentecost Has Come Again," and God confirmed His Word by filling ten with the Holy Ghost, four men, three women and three children. One of the women saved formerly taught girls to dance for the Devil Bush Society. As the natives prayed with tears streaming down their nude breasts, she purposed in her heart they would have dresses, even if she must divide her meager supply with them. She forgot her misery in the rich blessings except when cutting abdominal pains nearly doubled her over the pulpit.

By Monday morning, with a temperature of 103°, it was evident the new missionary had malaria—an old enemy of West African Missions. The family at Maheh was deeply concerned, prayed for her often and the senior girls bathed her constantly to keep the fever down. Willie went to the bush and brought beautiful red flowers for the patient.

Wednesday, Kenny started for Monrovia to send a cable home requesting prayer and post a letter from Georgia to Marie.

> *I'm sorry to write you that your mother has malaria. She hasn't been well for a week, on Monday she had a chill and her temperature was 105° by night.*
>
> *We are doing everything possible for her—the things I think you would do if you were here. I love her dearly and will do my best to help her. The children love her very much, too, and are praying for her continually. They are willing helpers.*
>
> *Since her fever was high again last night, I am sending for advice from a doctor in Monrovia and cabling you at the same time.*
>
> *I'll keep you posted, but believe your mother will be better in a few days.*
>
> *Let Carmen and your brother know.*

Nancy Ann massaged her neck and shoulders with prayer and falling tears. Rebecca and Gladys helped Georgia to bathe her frequently.

Thursday, Simon returned from a twenty four hour walk to Suehn with three bottles of ice. She looked at it with glassy eyes, lifted it up and praised God for it. She wanted to rub it on her fevered face, look at it and drink water with ice floating on it, all at once.

Issac started for Monrovia Friday to send another cable.

> *"Mother improving, Keep praying will not wire again unless worse."*

Kenny returned with seven letters for her, two from Marie, one from Carmen, one from her father, the rest from friends—splendid tonic for a sick lady! She felt rich and materially blest. Jacob's mother came to see her, "God will help you, because you have come to help us," she said.

The workmen and villagers came by with a strictly Liberian expression of sympathy,

"Never mind, yah!"

She slept for short intervals and wakened reaching for more ice water—seemed to hear voices lifted in prayer all night long. Georgia put a jar of boiled water in the river to cool. Arnon David came in with a tearful apology,

"Mother Robinson, I 'met' a can of water in the river. I didn't know what it was, so I poured it out and got me some raw water to drink. Then the boys told me it was your water I met, I'm sorry."

A comical quartet all under six years old, came to serenade her Sunday afternoon. Sandra, Moses, Daniel and Lawrence accompanied their pleasant singing with many contortions—rolling eyes, patting feet and heads jerking from side to side. Homemade cheer for the convalescent.

Regaining her strength was a slow tedious process. One afternoon as they rested in hammocks slung in the the big kitchen, Gladys asked plaintively,

"Am I a full-fledged missionary yet, Reggie?"

"You're learning, Robbie, dear," answered Georgia with a sympathetic smile, "learning fast."

Chapter 6

PALAVER!

'Palaver' is an apt Liberian word used to describe everything from minor problems and disagreements to murder trials. No matter how small the village there is always a palaver kitchen. Gladys found later they were excellent beginning places to introduce the Gospel but she chafed with impatience under many extended, verbose palavers first. She soon learned they were an absolute necessity for settling arguments, clearing the air, and getting to the bottom of tricky situations.

Not long after her recovery from malaria they noticed that the promising spirit of revival had vanished. Services were bound, worship stilted and dry, as if the young people went through the motions without reality. Puzzled and sad they fasted and prayed, and were amazed at the simple situation that triggered the answers.

Eddie came with a palaver; someone had taken his eddoes (edible root tubers from a large leafed plant.) When they questioned the family trying to find the culprit, several told of other's misdeeds. A few admitted their guilt, but there was very little contrition. Gladys gave a stern message.

"God cannot bless us—there is too much sin in the camp."

The palaver grew. One would plead guilty, then implicate his campanions in sin. Each one had to be dealt with personally. All other activities on the mission ceased. From morning until night there was palaver for a week that would afterwards be remembered as the "Black Week." Confessions poured out as a filthy stream. Some misdemeanors dated back to the time of the Haneys. The ladies felt weak and heartsick, wondered how much more they could stand and if saints at home were praying for them. They continually cried out,

"More grace, Lord, more grace!"

Gladys wrote her children a note,

> *"I've regained what I lost with malaria. We are having spiritual warfare plenty. No time for a real letter—ask everyone to pray for us."*

Slowly, the road led upward again. There was genuine conviction and repentance, though some rebelled. They prayed for guidance in meting out suitable punishment. Issac was asked to leave permanently. Four others left rather than accept their chastisement but returned early the next morning begging to be punished and restored to the family. Their request was granted. Everyone was called together to hear the reinforced rules and warned of the consequence of disobedience in the future. Those who had made mistakes were put on a six months proof period.

By the next Sunday, the whole atmosphere was changed. Many of the young people stood voluntarily and with contrition asked forgiveness publicly for the wrongs done. Gladys declared,

"As Ezra of old, we could not lift up our faces for the sin around us. The devil tried to tear up the mission, but with true repentance, we have victory again, Halleujah!" With her words a wave of blessing rolled over the assembly and tears were changed to rejoicing.

The promise of revival burned brighter than before and she was able to thank God for palaver—how ever painful.

Chapter 7

BOX 44

Gladys took the afternoon off and went to the new house to relax and answer mail. This was her first opportunity to write the long newsy letters she felt her family deserved.

I'm so thankful to hear the Berean class has sent packages. They will be a great blessing.

Reggie plans to go to Monrovia the 3rd of November. We hope our checks will be there from Headquarters, otherwise won't be able to mail the letters I'm writing.

(I wish the lizard running around my feet would run on out of the room!)

I've had Moses sitting by himself under a palm tree all morning for punishment. He had his hands up pretending to talk in tongues at church. One of the big boys shook him and told him to stop, he answered with some very ugly words. His other offence was meddling in the teacher's kitchen, which is out of bounds.

It's 7:30 p.m. now. (I'll write in installments as

I get a chance) We went to the chapel to study John chapter seven a short while ago. A storm came up, blew out our light and filled the church with dust. We knew rain was coming so ran for the house—hard rain pelted us on the way. I don't know how it happened but when we got to our doorstep, I was still holding little Moses by the hand. He's very happy—thinks he will get to spend the night with us.

Next Day

Well, it rained so hard he did spend the night at the mission house, but he's been in trouble again and is now back under his palm tree doing time!

Nashville Sunday School sent a check for $67.75. Thank God! It was desperately needed. I can only pray God's blessings on them and write a letter that cannot halfway express my gratitude.

A man brought a dressed-out deer to sell to us, we bought all we thought we could use before it would spoil. We are going to try frying some like beefsteak. Beefsteak! Where have I heard that word before? I told Reggie to cream potatoes and make cabbage slaw to eat with it—two more strange items here.

p.s. The deer steak was good and tender—we enjoyed it without potatoes and slaw.

p.s. no. 2 Did I tell you I lost eighteen pounds while I was sick? I've already put it on again.

Another afternoon in the new house and several letters were ready to go. When Gladys wrote the return address neatly in the upper left corner of the envelopes she looked at the line *Box 44, Monrovia,* and realized for the first time the strategic role of that postal box.

"My life revolves around it," she mused, "even though I spend my days in mission work, the deep longing to hear from my children is always with me. It's a comfort that Marie and Allan have companions—little Rita Joy is added joy—but, I left my Baby at such a tender age, only seventeen.

Oh Carmen, I hope you are happy at the Tulsa school—I read over and over the sweet letters you write, and ache for more.

I don't hear from Allan often, but Verla writes. Precious, faithful Marie keeps the letters coming. Then, there are friends, and Dad, and God's wonderful family, the fruit of Box 44 gladdens my heart and brightens my days in a way nothing else could.

To think, this has been the address of Pentecostal missionaries in Liberia for several decades—our only avenue of contact with the rest of the world. Someday telephone service will be freely available, but now, we depend on Box 44, as the receiving end of a vast, tenuous umbilical cord. Through its small door issues money for expenses supplies and building, exciting package notices, envelopes brimming with love and official letters that say, Maybe, if, or No, retrench, or Yes, proceed. There's sad news, joyful tidings, disappointments and encouragement, not to mention surprises of every dimension.

The innocent appearing cubicle whose exact location and size have varied with remodeling and building operations over the years all too often has an invisible label reading "Hole of Disappointment" or maybe, "Hope Deferred."

On the other hand, all the news, needs, longings and happenings on the field leave with the Box 44 autograph. It's awesome and almost frightening to consider all that will yet come and be sent under its auspices.

She shivered with a quick flash of premonition, then reminded herself, "One step at a time, in Jesus' Name. That's how I'll make it," and settled back in her chair to reread the well worn missiles that Jack brought from his last trip to town.

Box 44

Box 44 is still used by Missionaries Jimmie Hall and Nona Freeman.

Box 47 is still used by Missionaries Jimmie Hall and Norma Freeman.

Chapter 8
VARMINTS, ETC.

"Varmints" as Gladys called them made regular appearances. One Sunday a scorpion capable of a lethal sting was killed at church, the next, Jack discovered a snake parked on the rafters. Azmona climbed a pole and punched him, he hit the floor running, but gleeful, concerted effort put him out of action. When she asked if it was poisonous, the boys answered,

"Um-m, plenty bad!"

They told her about killing a boa constrictor at Beajah with sixty eggs in it.

"How big were the eggs?" she asked.

"Oh! Big past chicken eggs!"

Speaking of chicken eggs, there were plenty of them on the menu—two for breakfast, four chicken-egg custard for lunch, and often boiled ones for supper. There was a large glass of orange juice for each meal plus the canned vegetables bought from Pettys. Occasionally, the villagers brought okra and tiny bitter tomatoes they could buy. The hearts of young palm trees called palm cabbage made good salad, but, their fare was mostly monotonous. Georgia hoped to find some variations on the next trip to town. Bananas were plentiful, sometimes they could hardly face another one! Their garden gave feeble promise due to lack of humus and extremes of either rain or sun.

The children expected rice with every meal—did not think they had eaten without it. Whatever they ate with rice was called 'soup'. Soup could consist of many or few ingredients—tender cassava leaves, okra, hot peppers, tomatoes, onions, wild greens, venison, fish or monkey. Pounded cassava, yams and plaintains were side dishes. Whatever the meal was concocted of, it was always called 'chop'.

Mother Holmes came for a weekend. Gladys felt a kindred spirit with the dynamic little lady from Zordee on their first meeting.

Monday morning, after they lovingly waved good-bye to Mother Holmes when she started down the trail going home, Georgia and Gladys took six of the young men on a small expedition. They climbed a high hill on a narrow path cut by laborers from Bomi Hill mine to an observation point on the top. It was so steep in places, Jack and Jason pulled them up by one hand while they grabbed handholds on vines and branches with the other one. Poles were laid across the path for steps where it slanted sharply upward. Extreme exertion to get there was amply rewarded by a breathtaking view.

They could see deserted Beajah on the other side of thick jungle. Red roofed Maheh brightened the whole landscape, edged by Maheh river glinting silver in the soft light of a partly cloudy day. It appeared to nestle neat and lovely in a valley, though actually it sat on a hill!

Miles to the north was the iron ore hill called Bomi where mining was beginning slowly with hopes of full scale operation later. As Gladys looked that direction she felt a strange tug on her heart that she did not understand until afterward.

They were thirsty after the climb and had forgotten to take boiled drinking water. Jason showed them God's provision for travellers—large water vines all along the trail. The boys cut pieces two or three feet long and tilted them so the cool water flowed directly into their waiting mouths. They decided it must be pure sealed inside the sections of the vine. Jason warned

"There's another vine that looks the same but the water is bitter. There's only one true water vine."

Alfred killed two monkeys on the return trip, so the children had 'sweet chop' the next day.

Gladys received letters that the Berean class, Brother and Sister Dugan and Marie had mailed boxes of clothing for the children. She collared Moses and told him about the new clothes on the way,

"If those nice people knew how you neglect to clean your plate, they would send that nice suit to some other little boy."

He stood there forlornly holding his rusty metal plate with tears making tiny black trails on his dusty cheeks. Georgia whispered,

"I wish we had a picture of him the way he looks right now."

They comforted him, then told him about the 'dash' (prize or tip in Liberian vernacular) they planned to give the children who kept their plates shiny clean until Christmas. They hinted it might be a red balloon, (the Haneys wrote they were sending some).

Moses was late for prayer meeting that night—he was down at the river scrubbing his plate with sand. 7:00 a.m. the next morning he was back on the river bank scouring the plate again whose appearance was much improved.

The ladies decided to dash the group working on the air strip to see if it couldn't be speeded up a bit!

Daniel was another four year old, not as mischievious as Moses, but, a perfect mimic. Ordinarily sweet and well-mannered, when singing he seemed transformed into whomever he imitated with every gesture and mannerism true to life. It was hard to keep a straight face when each chorus reflected a different easily recognized personality.

As Gladys taught an evening Bible Study, she wondered why the young men kept asking basic questions about the plan of salvation that they had been drilled in over and over. Afterward, they told her a Moslem was present and they wanted him to hear the answers. He was a brother to Momo, one of the finest young men raised on the Mission. She was thrilled with their burden and concern for this soul.

She was taking pictures one Sunday afternoon when a stranger asked if she would take a picture of him with his snake. Without a second thought she agreed. He soon returned with a green spotted one about five feet long and she snapped him with the snake twined around his body and legs. He looked so harmless she got gentle and asked Georgia to take one of her holding the snake's tail. Then Sammie Gessi, one of the workmen told her,

"It's a very poisonous snake. He uses witchcraft to keep it from biting him."

She was annoyed because the thing was brought on the mission among the wide-eyed children, and with herself for complying with his request. She ordered the man to leave the grounds immediately with his snake.

Mother Holmes came by the next day, Georgia teased,

"Well, Mother, I guess we can call Gladys an oldtimer now. She's 'met' malaria, had a jigger in her toe and handled a snake!"

After they all laughed, Mother Holmes told her, "Child, I've been in Africa fifty years. You'll learn, as I did, not to try everything you see the natives do."

She shared some sad news,

"Remember Sister Jiles from the mission five days walk from here? Her health has failed, she must return home, and there's no one to continue her work."

They grieved together recalling the words of Jesus, "Laborers are few."

November, Monday, the 10th, 1947 Gladys wrote her children,

I'm alone with the children on the Mission. Reggie left early for Monrovia—looks like this will be a lonely week. Some excitement I could

do without, the children just killed a dangerous, hairy black spider a few inches from Mary Ruth's head.

Bandy Boy and Sammie Gessi, workmen who sleep in the village, came just after Reggie left and announced there was a big palaver in the village. (I almost dodge at the word.) When I heard the seriousness of the matter I called everyone to the chapel and we prayed for guidance. The young people felt I should be present when the matter is brought before the chief.

November 11th

I went. The palaver began 'plenty' serious in the kitchen with the chief swinging in his hammock, but soon proceedings were interrupted by an excited messenger. A man has been attacked by a Lion monkey and his arm badly mangled. A lot of uninterpreted chatter followed—finally, the palaver was resumed. A more important Chief arrived, evidently held in high respect. He was friendly and spoke excellent English.

Then a boy and a girl ran yelling toward the river; a commotion followed them. Palaver recessed! Jason interpreted. 'They say a canoe is coming up from the bottom of the river—a mysterious thing.' We followed the crowd. "There it is!" they said and pointed to the opposite bank. A man jumped in a canoe, rowed across and pulled a large plank from the water.

Many were disappointed. They thought this was going to be definite proof of the legendary "water people" they believe live under the water. Jason sniffed, "That's the way they get all that stuff. Someone imagines something and tells it and they all believe it."

The crowd returned to the kitchen and the palaver continued, much the same as court in America, only prolonged. After five hours a decision was reached and the guilty ordered to pay stiff fines. The Big Chief explained the whole proceedings fully to me. Most interesting.

Gladys expected Georgia back on Friday or Saturday and as prearranged had hammock men and eight carriers for loads waiting for her. The hammock men returned on Sunday without her. She sent them back with implicit instructions to wait until Georgia got there. She was afraid the carriers might return too, so divided the small stock of rice and sent half by two more carriers with the same orders.

Meanwhile, they were out of soap and money, and down to two small cans of milk for the babies. Gladys stopped giving Ruth and Johanna milk earlier, as they were older. They were eating mashed bananas, egg custard, orange juice and country bread (pounded rice cereal).

While missionary Gladys was writing letters, student Gladys came to her,

"Mudder, the rice, it is finish."

"If so," Gladys answered, "I'm leaving." All those

mouths waiting to be fed recognized nothing as food if rice was missing. The student followed the missionary to the storehouse laughing. Sure enough, it was 'finish', but the missionary decided to stay and borrow from the tithes to buy more rice. She thought,

"When Reggie returns with some Mission funds, we'll feel rich—if they've come."

There were mercies. Since the rains had slacked, the boys were able to catch some delicious fish. She made a delightful discovery—the garden she thought would never produce had okra and green beans ready to eat.

Except for mealtimes and short rest periods she watched three grasscutters slinging their hooks all day Tuesday. These were boys between ten and twelve years old and masters of the slick disappearing act if she glanced away.

7:00 p.m. Tuesday, Georgia returned. Everyone went out to welcome her, prayer meeting was called off as excitement ran high. All gathered around to see what she had brought. There was food—the babies could be "full plenty" again—a few choice delicacies as canned cheese and bacon, and disappointments. No letters from home and no mission funds. Georgia had stayed the extra days haunting Box 44, but this was one of those "Hope Deferred" times. Together, they thanked God for the Sunday school offering sent by Brother Dugan which bought the groceries.

Four days later Kenny came late from Monrovia with mail, two letters from Marie and one from

Carmen helped brace her against the shocking news written in a letter to both ladies. The Haneys would not be returning to Liberia.

"Oh Reggie," Georgia whispered, "This means our airstrip and hope of a plane has gone up in smoke! We'll have to keep struggling and traveling by hammock and by foot. I can't help feeling heartsore, but the Lord knows best—let's pray."

Those prayers were well-moistened with tears, and continued until early morning.

Chapter 9

VILLAGES BEYOND

Momo, Jack, Paul S., Jason, Little Issac, Gladys, Nancy Ann, Dorcas and Naomi went with Gladys to Weahama for a service—the first ever held there. It was an hour's walk requiring constant vigilance to avoid tripping over roots, rocks and fallen limbs. They crossed three creeks on treacherous logs, but returned rejoicing. The people were interested and appreciative.

"We'll build a 'church kitchen' if you'll come every Saturday. We want to hear more," they said.

November 27th she wrote her children:

> *"I've suddenly realized this is Thanksgiving Day. Our dinner was fish, okra, corn, spinach and fruit salad and we were thankful, but without a special Thanksgiving feeling. I don't think we'll be able to 'feel' Christmas either, but will have a Christmas Dinner and try.*
>
> *A group of the children and I climbed the Scenie Hill again. Reggie couldn't go with us—has a sprained ankle. She and I went for a canoe ride in the late afternoon, with Jason and Willie*

rowing for us. The river was dark and beautiful in the fading light, bordered by deep green jungle. Ahead of us a big crocodile hit the water with a splash. We had the gun so the boys rowed fast to get to the spot, but all we found were his tracks in the sand. We went to Maheh village, past the spot that was cleared for worship of the "Water People." It's growing up now, because the Gospel has been preached here.

There is some misunderstanding about my allotment from Headquarters, but Brother Dugan's Sunday school offering will tide me over until it's straightened out.

I've enjoyed studying the book of John with the young people. Gladys gave this account of Mary anointing Jesus;

"Mary took her sweet grease and rubbed it on Jesus." The triumphal entry; "The people took palm thatch and waved it."

This is the dry season and we are sweltering in heat, however, I rejoice—we can evangelize unhindered by heavy rains.

Pray for us

P.S. We have romance on the mission, Gladys and Jason are engaged. Nancy Ann and Jack wanted to be, but we have asked them to wait 'small.'

The next service at Weahama was exciting! The Chief and several men digging for gold at the creek returned for the meeting.

"This is a Moslem village, but we have hungry hearts," was the comment.

Gladys, native pastor

Jason preached with unction. When she spoke, Gladys declared, "Mohammed cannot save, so Jesus has sent us to tell you about Him."

Before the end of her message a wave of conviction swept the whole assembly to their knees, crying to God for mercy. A tradesman in witchcraft wept, asking Jesus to take evil out of his heart. The small band left with great joy. The Chief gave them yams and country bread and with many people escorted them part of the way home.

Every Sunday afternoon Georgia took most of the young people with her to Mannah, a nearby village. They reported growing interest in the services there.

Gladys tackled Kowadee next, Jim's home village, much larger than Weahama. Jason, Momo, Davis, the two Ernests, Gladys, Willie, Jack and Nancy Ann accompanied her rowing up a lonely river to the first small settlement. On the way, Nancy Ann screamed when a crocodile plunged from a low limb to the water beside the canoe. Student Gladys stepped on the box they sat on. It broke through and only a quick helping hand saved her from a dunking!

A young mother pounding rice for country bread greeted them warmly. Gladys asked if she knew Jesus. She looked puzzled and answered, "No." Gladys wanted to pause long enough to tell the needy woman the sweet story, but they were hurrying to many others who had not heard either and a messenger had gone ahead to announce their arrival.

They traveled through rice fields, bush and jungles for two hours, fording three streams. Twice they saw bush cow tracks (buffaloes). Gladys was thankful not to meet personally the makers of the tracks. They had four encounters with driver ants. Once she got a shoe full that had to be picked off one at a time. They climbed over waist high tree trunks.

Kowadee was clean-swept with a small lovely Moslem Temple near the town kitchen where the people gathered. The Chief welcomed them graciously and she responded with gratitude. They sang choruses in Gola and she preached I Timothy 3:16, "God was manifested in the flesh." The Spirit did not allow her to stumble for words! When she gave an invitation to repent, the Chief was the first to kneel and all the people followed his example.

After prayer there was much earnest palaver in Gola.

"Are they pleased or displeased?" she questioned Jason.

"Pleased,"

"The Chief has a request," Jason replied. "Will you come every Saturday and teach us about Jesus."

She felt if she considered the difficulties of the trip and refused, their blood would drip from her fingers in the judgment.

"Yes," she promised, "We will come."

A large group followed them out of town. She felt Calvary love for all of them, and with the final greeting hugged the women with tears streaming down her face.

"We'll see you next Saturday!" they kept calling.

She thrilled to her helpers singing, "Take the whole world, but give me Jesus," on the return journey. The walked single file down the jungle trail and their songs seemed to weave a canopy of sweet sound that echoed from the greenery. They reached the mission after 4:00 p.m., tired, hungry, thirsty and happy!

The second week of December, Dorcas, Gladys and Victoria helped the missionaries with a major kitchen clean-up in the Mission house. They took up tatters of worn-out linoleum and scrubbed the shelves and board floors until they shone. While working they talked of the villages and how they needed God's power to reach them.

"The Lord's been dealing with me about prayer and fasting—I believe it's our answer," Georgia shared.

Gladys was excited, "That's exactly what I feel!"

Many of the young people were moved to join the missionaries in a three-day fast. They felt the results on the Saturday circuit. Remarkable healings happened in response to simple prayer. The town kitchens overflowed with repenting people.

One Saturday on the way to Kowadee they stopped at Bougbai to witness—the spiritual hunger of the folk compelled them to return again and again. A converted devotee of witchcraft asked plaintively,

"Can't you come to see us one day when you don't have to 'hurry on'?"

Gladys promised to stay as long as possible on the next visit, but 'hurrying on' was the only answer to the urgency she felt to reach the villages.

She was thankful for many packages that came—they would make the Christmas palaver easier. She found her human heart still divided. Part of her longed to be with loved ones, yet there was deep satisfaction that she and Georgia were privileged to lift up a light in the darkness. They hoped loving and giving would help the people around them to understand the loving Gift of Calvary. She longed to send gifts for her family, but the bit of personal money brought with her was quickly absorbed in the Mission. Her $60.00 a month allotment strained to whittle down the $175.00 food debt and meet personal needs.

The Christmas service, December the 21st, was blest and well attended by the town people. They gave gifts, candy, balloons and clothes. Everyone was excited and grateful. Georgia and a group went to Mannah service that afternoon while Gladys and two girls took turns caring for sick crying babies. She was deeply disappointed when no one came from town for the night service.

"The Devil Bush Society has opened and no females are allowed out after sundown. Even in the daytime they must hide if the 'country devil' is near. This thing breaks up the Sunday night service every year. The head of the Society lives in Maheh village," Jason explained.

"Then, tomorrow morning you'll go with me to see that Headman. I'll not be silent when God's work suffers," Gladys answered.

Jason agreed, although he understood better than she did the awe and dread these men inspired. Rachel walked with them to the village. Gladys and Jason confronted the Headman.

"Sir," she said, "We have come 8,000 miles to help your people. Now, because of your activities, they are afraid to come to church on Sunday nights. I request that you stop hindering the women, and make it possible for the folk to worship God."

Her audacity so surprised the man that he meekly acquiesced. She thanked him graciously and left his house praising God.

Before leaving the village she stood with several women and children watching a man kill a poisonous snake in a banana tree. Suddenly, a horrible scream came from the woods where a Devil Bush Society was in session. Instantly, every woman vanished, even Rachel who stood beside her. She watched them trembling as they covered their doors with mats and thought,

"Poor duped women! It's all built up to mysterious proportions to keep them in fear."

This was the "Heart Men" season, too. No one traveled alone. These anonymous men were paid to collect human hearts, and frequently other organs of the body. Who paid was a mystery, but the why was without doubt witchcraft. Georgia appealed to the Government for protection of young men from the Mission on their regular necessary trips to Monrovia.

"Send two at a time, and they must identify themselves by continually blowing a whistle whenever they leave the Mission Compound," was the answer.

Against this somber background, the ladies tried to make Christmas a spiritual and happy time for the Mission family. Gladys felt a little Christmas spirit when she walked out on Christmas Eve morning and saw palm branch arches made by Ernest and Joe and decorated with velvety red balls from the jungles. But, the tropical heat quickly dissolved the illusion. Since Satan observes no holidays, he chose to make that a hard day in more than one way.

When all the children came to the Mission house in the evening to sing carols, the ladies saw the girls had displayed pictures of their children in prominent places and decorated them with fresh flowers. This thoughtful kindness unwittingly aggravated holiday homesickness. Veteran Georgia blinked and kept a stiff upper lip, but greenhorn Gladys gave way to a flood of tears. When she saw the children's sad faces and remembered how much she wanted to help Georgia build a pleasant, godly home life for them, she dried her eyes and forced herself to smile.

They sang, prayed and read the Christmas story. Thanks to folk in America everyone received gifts, candy, popcorn, balloons and clothes. Games were played with lots of running and laughing under the full tropical moon aided by a gasoline lantern to brighten shadowy places.

Christmas Day was to be a day of rest. They planned their menu with the benefits of those wonderful packages; chicken with oyster dressing, lima beans, palm cabbage salad, pickles, olives, fruit salad from home-grown fruits and three kinds of cake, chocolate, coconut and the fruit cake sent by Marie. The children anticipated plenty 'monkey chop,' their choice.

However, before dinner was ready, people from the village arrived. More came—they kept coming. No service was planned for Christmas Day, but, so many came they could not miss the chance to preach to these Moslems about God coming to earth, manifesting Himself in Jesus, who died and rose again to purchase salvation for all mankind.

After the message the altar filled with seekers, weeping and praying, but, some of the Mission boys were restless and disturbed the prayer service. Evidently, their minds were on the 'monkey chop.' For recompense they received a severe scolding and were fined twenty five cents each. All the villagers not present the previous Sunday expected a Christmas gift. It took some scratching to find a small thing for everyone.

3:00 p.m. they sat down to cold Christmas dinner, too weary to enjoy the extra treats. Sore muscles from game-playing and the inevitable longing for their families pressed too close for comfort.

December 27th Diary

Kowadee again! We had a good service at Bougbai on the way. They insist, "Please keep coming, and tell us more."

I'm so glad for Saturdays! I love all these people and am anxious for works to be established everywhere, but Kowadee is especially on my heart. My God is big enough to work that whole town over!

Everyone was glad to see us, I preached,

"What shall it profit a man if he gain the whole world and lose his own soul." God moved on the people's hearts and they were deeply stirred.

After service, a woman brought us rice and fish soup. We were tired and hungry (never take time to prepare food for these trips.) I was determined to show my appreciation for their kindness, so took a hair out of the soup and ate it. Though blazing hot with pepper, it was good. They were pleased and the children were happy that I ate their 'country chop.'

Dodyie, who worked for the Mission occassionally, came to borrow $6.00. Georgia thought he had country cloth to pawn, asked him to bring it so they could see. He came back with a small, black male goat and declared it was a milk goat that Mother Regenhardt promised to buy. Plenty of goat palaver but no money loaned!

Ruthie's mother and father came to visit. Her mother lifted her bandana and showed Gladys a pitiful baby beneath it, only four days old. Its mother was dying and the baby had not been fed. Though she gave them powdered milk for it, they felt disappointed that the missionaries could not take the baby.

January 3rd, 1948 Gladys confided in her diary.

Today my son is twenty one years old. How I would like to be with him, his wife, and that sweet baby I've never seen. I've thought back to his babyhood and childhood until I'm terribly homesick to see him. I wish he would write more often.

Many asked to be baptized at Kowadee on their next visit. She requested they wait 'small'—to be sure they fully understood the significance of taking the Name of Jesus in Baptism. Her message that day was hard against the sins rife in all the villages; witchcraft, drinking, adultery, gambling, and murder. Sincere repentant prayer with tears afterward made her rejoice but the words of the Chief let her heart overflow, "We have agreed together to build a church for a place to worship Jesus."

Her tears were tears of joy. Jack said,

"I'm happy too much!"

Unfortunately, among the sincere and hungry, there are also schemers of evil designs. A woman came begging Gladys to visit her village. She claimed her people wanted to hear the gospel and she would personally guide her there. Gladys could not understand the odd reluctance she felt—reaching the lost was her burden—after all! The woman was persuasive and though her usual helpers could not accompany them, she agreed to go.

They walked for many hours. On reaching the village after dark, the Chief greeted her coolly,

"It's too late for church now, you can have a service tomorrow morning."

She was weary enough not to mind, thinking.

"I'll be fresher tomorrow and have more strength—"

They gave her food then led her to the hut where

Headman

she would sleep. A strange uneasiness encircled her as she entered. The sleeping mat was not on the customary platform but lay flat on the floor. There was a peculiar gaping hole low in the opposite wall.

She prayed longer than usual before turning on her stomach to sleep. She was wakened in the night by something extremely heavy and cold lying across the middle of her back. The lantern she left burning was out, and chills of fear rippled over her in the darkness. Though her heart pounded, she tried to lay very still while her whole soul cried silently to the Lord for help.

"In the Name of Jesus, in the Name of Jesus!" Her lips formed the words. Slowly the heavy object slid off and she heard dragging movement on the mud floor as it left the room.

When she emerged from the hut early the next morning there was instant consternation. She figured it out in the night—this village on the riverbank worshiped a huge crocodile. She was brought by guile for the sacrifice to their "god." It didn't work, thank God! Everything else put on the mat was dragged to the river and eaten by the loathesome creature.

They couldn't believe she was alive. The woman who brought her fell terrified at her feet begging forgiveness. Gladys sternly demanded that all the people come together so she could talk to them. She pointed out the powerlessness of their god and declared in ringing tones how Jesus, the Almighty One, delivered her and wanted to save them.

She gave them the plan of salvation in detail from

the promise to fallen man in Eden, to the birth of the church on the day of Pentecost. The spirit held the people spellbound. When she invited them to repent, the haughty Chief was the first to kneel and the rest followed his example.

The biggest shock of all was learning this village was actually near Maheh. The woman said it was far away and led Gladys on a wild walk around and around the jungle—still, Jesus brought good out of evil. She knew all who cried and prayed would not pay the price to serve the Lord but was confident some would. They did and in time a church was established, Halleujah!

January 7th, Wednesday, Diary

Jack brought a message from Maheh—his uncle's baby was very ill. According to their custom they mourned with loud wails because they thought it would not live through the night. This is a family that has rejected God all the years the Mission has been here, but now, they want prayer. Reggie went to see them and said the parents could bring the baby to the Mission for a few days, if they remove the charms and witch medicine. They called the Chief and town people who agreed we should try to help them.

We prayed for the baby, washed some of the filth from its head and body and put on its first diaper and gown, afraid to tire it too much. We put a baby bed in the living room and it rested and seemed better for awhile. At nine p.m. the baby began to cry as though it suffered. We prayed again and again. Gladys went with the mother to call her husband. She still thought the witches wanted to eat her baby, but both of them prayed everytime we did. We sent for Jack. The baby was quieter but felt cold, so we warmed blankets to cover it. Gladys helped me while Jack and the parents were on their knees. Midnight I saw the baby was too still and very cold, I called Reggie. We looked at each other, "What do you think?" I whispered. "I think—you'd better tell them we did all we could," she answered.

I went to the parents and told them what she said and that Jesus had taken their baby to live with Him. I put my arms around the mother as I spoke, but neither of them moved or said a word. I tried again, "Your baby isn't suffering anymore. Its spirit is now with Jesus waiting for you to come live with Him there."

There wasn't a sound from either of them, but the man began to tremble so I knew he understood the baby was dead. Both of us tried to comfort them. Finally, the man spoke, "I know you did your best. If the baby had not been here, it wouldn't have lived this long."

At one o'clock we still sat as though stunned. We felt so helpless, no undertaker, no telephone calls, no coffin, no preparation. At last, the father said they wanted to take the baby back to town. Just as it was dressed, we wrapped the body in a white sheet, pinned it, then put a white blanket around it. Momo said he couldn't carry the body, his toes were too sore. Jason hesitated, then picked it up and led the small group down the jungle path to the village a mile away—a long procession walking by dim lantern light.

We cringed to think of the cruel accusations the town people would bring against them—they had "made witch" and caused the baby's death and now the witches would eat it. More than ever we realized how securely these people are bound by the devil with superstition and fear. We went to bed with heavy hearts, our only comfort, "Our God doeth all things well," and He knows what is best. Later, we heard loud mourning from the town.

January 8th, Thursday

Jack sent a note from the village, his uncle wanted us to come before they buried the baby. Reggie and I went, leaving Nancy Ann in charge of the Mission. When we entered their hut, men sat on mats in the first room. I walked through looking for the mother. The next room was dark, I saw the litle white bundle laying on a bamboo mat just in time to keep from stepping on it. We found the mother doubled up on the mat in the following room weeping bitterly for her baby.

Reggie asked the Chief to call the people together so we could talk to them. They gathered in the town kitchen and laid the small mat with its burden before our chairs. The mother sat on a tiny stool at the baby's head and the father near its feet. Such a strange funeral—Christian rites are unknown in most of the villages.

The children sang two choruses in Gola and I preached an evangelistic message warning against witchcraft and God's judgment. Both of us admonished and comforted the parents, then dismissed. Women are not allowed to see a burial, but after I left the kitchen, I looked back and saw two men swinging the little body between them in a cloth. Though the baby was four months old, it had not been named. They buried it in a grave about two feet deep to await the resurrection. The Lord will have people from every nation, even if it has to be little ones like this from the heathen lands.

January 9th, Friday

The mother of the baby came to the Mission this morning and asked us to pray for her. Reggie showed her a picture of Jesus with little children. We tried again to comfort her, and she drank in every word. Our hearts ached for her, broken-hearted and afraid, tortured by age-old superstition.

Gladys realized her baby would soon be eighteen years old. She sent money ahead of time to her friends, the Grahams.

"Buy a pretty cake," she wrote, "put eighteen candles on it, and have it waiting in her room the night before her birthday with the candles lit and a nice card signed, 'with all my love, from Mother.' " She couldn't do more.

A five day evangelistic tour to Bomi Hills and Bolah with Jack, Jason, Ernest and Nancy Ann was hindered for ten days. She felt unable to walk so far and couldn't get hammock carriers. They promised twice and failed to come. She went to the village to see if persuasion would help. The Chief said the men had sore arms from vaccinations. She discerned there would be other excuses when their arms were well. Walking back from Maheh defeated, the thought came, "A day's walk can't hurt my body more than leaving my loved one's hurt my heart—."

"Jack, you and Ernest go to the Mission, tell Jason and Nancy Ann to come and bring our luggage and supplies. Hurry! We're going."

She talked with Jesus while she waited by the trail and was assured of traveling mercy.

Jerry's father welcomed them at Bomi Hills with a white chicken. An ancient tradition of Liberia is the 'white thing'—a white gift expressing gratitude. He told them he prayed daily for someone to come hold regular services at the camp, and gave them good news. The Mining Company was building a road from Monrovia to Bomi Hills. Gladys rejoiced! Since her tedious arrival at the Mission, her prayers always included this plea, "Oh Lord, we need roads to reach this land." Now, it was beginning to happen! They promised another meeting on their return trip.

Walking was rough—their necks ached from looking down for safe places to step. They crossed three wide swamps on poles laid end to end. They met a man returning from a hippopotamus hunt with a large basket of the blubbery meat on his head. They went through coffee plantations and reached Bolah at 5:30 p.m.

They set down their loads in front of a neat house with a spacious front porch and waited while Ernest went to ask for a place to stay. A man returned with him and said,

"You may stay here. It belongs to a 'civilized' lady who has moved to a nearby village." All of them hoped to be given that house so took possession joyfully. There were two home-made bedsteads and an old table in the largest room. The young people made it home-like in a few moments with a cloth on the table, Gladys' cot set up with the mosquito net hanging over it and a bed made for Nancy. The boys arranged their room at the opposite end of the porch.

The owner of their temporary home, Mrs. Marshall, came for the night service and told them afterwards,

"Three times before, some came to preach here, but I've never seen the people so stirred."

The crowd wouldn't leave until Gladys promised a sunrise service before they went to the fields to work the next day. She talked with Mrs. Marshall until very late. The woman told that she loved the Lord and wanted to work for Him but never had heard before about people receiving the Holy Ghost today just as it was poured out on the day of Pentecost.

Many people came for the early service, Ruthie's father and mother among them. Their village was not far away. He asked to speak.

"We have come to church!"

"We didn't know about church last night, so we were not here. But, in the night I dreamed I saw a group dressed in white singing and worshiping Jesus. When I wanted to join them I was hindered, but did not give up. Finally I stood with the singers in a white robe too. My wife followed my example and great happiness came to us. I stand to renounce the Moslem religion, from today I will pray to Jesus only. Five times I sacrificed all my money and cloth to Allah to save my babies from dying, but I buried all five of them. My last and only child is well and healthy living on the Mission where these folks live."

Two other men stood and testified of similar dreams and renounced Mohamedism. Heaven swept across the gathering and Mrs. Marshall hit the ground dancing and speaking in tongues. Between waves of blessing, she gasped, "I've never felt like this before."

Since God moved so mightily they decided to stay for two more services—that night and the following morning. During the day Gladys found a sick old lady huddled on a low bamboo bed before a smoldering fire in her dark hovel. She was pathetic, her only clothing a rag around her loins. Gladys moved with compassion put her arms around her and told her about the love of Jesus. Later, someone said the old woman was a leper with her toes and fingers gone, Gladys didn't notice in the dim light.

Nancy took her for a walk to see the creek the drinking water came from and was embarrassed—a nude man was bathing in the middle of it. She decided to bring drinking water when she returned, for return she must. The heart-hunger of the people touched her long before they asked her to come again.

February 3rd
Letter to Marie and her friends at Nashville.

We had a variation in our diet. Jason and Willie killed a crocodile. According to their custom, first, we called the Chief to destroy the gall bladder, then enjoyed big slices of white meat, like fish without bones.

Gladys and Nancy Ann are laughing about 'playing possum' on Reggie and me last night, they pretended to be asleep when we called them. The chickens started screeching about 2:00 a.m. We ran out with flashlights and the gun. Though I shot, we didn't see anything. An hour later it happened again, Reggie shot low enough to hit any critter two-legged or four, but we didn't find evidence of a hit.

Of course, we couldn't surprise an intruder, yelling, slamming doors, flashing lights and shooting guns. I told Reggie if we run into a leopard down there one night, we may learn to stay in the house!

Some of the women at Kowadee last week did what they have long wanted to do—felt of my skin. They were amazed when I showed them the untanned flesh under my sleeve, and surprised to learn my hose was not skin.

I snatch every chance to write you so I can have a letter ready to go on short notice. I'm writing this in the boat on the way to Kowadee with a lot of jerking and splashing. The sun is barely up, the water looks dark and is steaming. I told the young people, I suppose the mythical 'water people' are cooking breakfast—looks like smoke rising.

My helpers are becoming real workers. Gladys preached her first sermon at Kowadee last week, and the people trembled with conviction. Jason brought a fine message at Bolah. The Lord met with us again there Monday evening and Tuesday morning, three young men received the Holy Ghost. Several workers came from Bomi Hill mine. It's a two hour hazardous walk one way—men won't usually go through there at night because of the buffaloes.

Now, don't get excited Marie. We haven't seen any in the daytime and I try to avoid walking at night.

Do keep the prayers going up and the letters coming!

Time to leave the canoe and hit the trail.

The next Sunday thirteen came from Kowadee and were baptized at the Mission—first fruits! Jason and Jack answered the call of a village beyond Kowadee that wanted to hear the gospel. Meetings in Bomi Hills gained momentum, and Reggie reported a real move in Mannah. However, victories did not come without backsets. There was an unpleasant showdown again with the Devil Bush Society for terrorizing the women.

The newly baptized returned to Kowadee and faced stiff opposition from Moslems.

Ruthie took pneumonia, Gladys tended her with prayer and loving care all day and night Sunday—thankfully, she improved enough the Bomi Hills—Bolah schedule was met Monday and Tuesday as usual.

She visited the leper-lady on every trip. This time she took her a handful of sweet-scented coffee blossoms. The thoughtfulness and love shown made her willing to listen as Gladys carefully explained the plan of salvation, ending, "Ma, if you will call on Jesus, obey the gospel and be His child, someday you'll see again your five little sons who died when they were babies."

For the first time she cried and prayed.

Ruthie's mother brought word of the baby boy they brought to the mission just after Christmas. The powdered milk she gave them kept it alive, but now, it was dying. Gladys' soft heart suffered every time they refused the little ones complying with the Mission Board's policy, which she agreed was wisdom. She knew they sent them away to die and had to come to terms with her tender feelings and reality.

"$5.00 a month would buy this starving baby milk, neither she nor the foster parents had the money. If it was provided they still wouldn't know how to feed it." She thought in consolation,

"These little souls will go straight to the arms of Jesus when they die, but many thousands have reached the age of accountability and need to hear the gospel so they can be saved. We already have so many children on the mission that we are hindered in evangelizing. God helping me, I must use my strength to reach the lost ones.

February 25th

Dear Children,

I found four letters when I came home. One from you, Marie, Sister Holland, Sister Gruse who was at Beajah Mission for a while and Brother Phillip Tolstad, formerly at Tulsa school. Believe me, I appreciate the yield of Box 44 more than ever.

When we got to Bolah the women came running with out-stretched arms, as though we were away ten years instead of a week.

They had news for me. Ten of them were fishing and found a huge boa constrictor. One said, "We are trusting Jesus now, so let's kill that snake before it kills somebody." They attacked it with sticks and poles. Everytime it lifted its big head they knocked it down. When the snake was dead, they doubled and tied it to a pole about ten feet long to bring it back. Some of them said it was the largest ever seen here. They showed me the pole and their clubs. I couldn't help but laugh at the way they told their adventure. They said the snake meat scattered all over town. They not only eat it fresh, but dry some for future use.

We had services in the open—most wonderful yet. One elderly lady walked up and down praising Jesus. She said she raised many children, some of them are old, but she never heard of Jesus. She was so happy that at last the good news came.

Twenty were baptized, including Ruthie's parents. The old lady with leprosy and five others will be baptized next time. I brought her two dresses that came in a package from Nashville. I found some muslin and pieced it with the sugar sack you sent, Marie, to make a mattress cover. The boys filled it with dry grass for her.

She was overwhelmed with such luxury, couldn't stop crying and praising the Lord. All of us cried with her. I suggested we kneel and thank Jesus. I told her love provided these blessings for her—very small in comparison with His love that has made the beautiful heavens for His children, greater and richer than anything we have seen.

Three repented at Bomi Hill last night, each from a different tribe. Seven tribes are represented there and the mine is only beginning to get under way.

Jason and Jack came back from Kowadee very excited, they had services in three other places.

Well, I've dragged you all over the country in this letter, haven't I? I have probably sweat more than you did reading it. I tell the young people it takes blood and sweat to save these people. Jesus gave the blood and we do the sweating—I'm grateful for the opportunity to do it. Pray and write!

All my love,
Mother

p.s. Two requests: two inexpensive or used Bibles—one for Jack to preach from and one for Sister Marshall, and some aerosal bombs, fleas do not let us sleep.

Gladys stayed with the children while Reggie and some of the young people made a three-day evangelistic tour the last of February. Jason's brother came from up country and the young men were praying with him. Gladys looked up in time to see the soles of Jack's shoes as he shot head first through the palm leaf siding. He landed outside flat on his back still praising God. He rejoiced at the prayer meeting later! Jason was 'climbing high' so two or three boys held him while they removed his heavy brogan shoes. They were afraid he would step on their bare feet.

She told them to do their shouting at home for out on the battlefield in the new places they would have to fight the devil instead of rejoicing—that is, until the new converts were brought to the shouting ground.

Trying to reach as many places as possible, they planned a gospel merry-go-round that would allow the two missionaries to see each other only once or twice a week. Gladys leaving Sunday afternoon for Bolah, Bopolu, Bomi Hills and other towns in that area returning Thursday night or Friday morning.

Georgia visiting the villages where she found open doors the past Friday and Saturday. Jack and Jason's responsibility was the Kowadee circuit. A new venture for Gladys was taking a group to Maheh village for a Saturday night meeting. They would be together at the Mission on Sunday morning and Georgia would continue with Mannah services on Sunday afternoon.

February 28th—letter to her children.

Marie, the shoebag you sent is too pretty for dirty shoes, so I'm using it for a letter file. Your pocket is the fullest. I really appreciate all the letters I receive and read them over and over again.

I've just typed a four page report on the work to Brother Stairs and the effort has left me blank.

Thought you'd like to know the leper-lady at Bolah was baptized along with several others.

There was no chance to send the letter, March 2nd on her first trip to Monrovia, she continued

Our teacher did not return—I'm going to try to find another one. We left the Mission yesterday morning and came by hammock and foot to Suehn Mission. This is where the boys came for ice when I had malaria. They said they stopped school for everyone to pray when they heard how sick I was.

I thought I was back in America sitting there drinking ice water and coke. There was real

butter on the table and they gave me a delicious apple—my first one since I left home. Truly delicious!

Then we got in a truck and actually **rode** *down the road for an hour to Millsburg where we spent the night. Maybe you think I didn't have a sense of well-being sitting up there in that truck sailing down the road! Gladys came with me to have a tooth pulled, she was quite uneasy on the truck ride.*

I have an urgent need for strong arch support shoes—since mine are worn out, walking is very difficult.

Tell the girls at Sunday school I received the D.D.T. Bomb and I'm anxious for another flea to attack me when I get home.

It may be two weeks or longer before I have another chance to send a letter, so don't worry if you do not hear from me.

I love you all 'plenty'!

The second week of March, after Bolah and Bomi Hills, she went to a new village called Bugbay and created quite a sensation among the women and children who had never seen a white woman before. After she spoke to a packed-out kitchen, most of the people knelt for prayer. The Chief's summary was amusing. "Our parents never told us about cars, but now we are finding out about them. Neither did they tell us about Jesus. A white woman has brought us the news about Him—now, we must believe and start praying to Him."

A man from Ghessi country came by the Mission with a herd of beef cattle on his way to Monrovia. Though the thirty day trip made him quite thin, they bought a calf for $16.00, planning to fatten him for canning later. The Mission children thought he was a grand animal since there were no cattle in this region. They put him in the chicken pen for protection from leopards and the chickens flew out squawking in every direction. They were not acquainted with cows either, had to be caught and returned, one by one.

Two Morrocans visited the Mission frightening the children with their long white robes and stringy black hair. They claimed to be looking for relatives, however Gladys and Georgia suspected they had come to strengthen their Moslem brethren. The ladies emphatic witness about the omnipotence of Jesus may have encouraged their sudden departure to continue the search elsewhere. One called over his shoulder as they left, "Pray to Jesus for me, sometimes". "We will pray," answered Gladys, "but, remember He wants to hear from you too."

Momo went to waterside in the middle of March on the third attempt to bring the refrigerator, but failed to find enough helpers. The ladies shrugged, "Maybe one more try will do it."

Chapter 10

HOW THE DREAM CAME TRUE!

From the first time Gladys climbed the Scenie Hill and looked toward the Bomi range of Hills, something drew her that direction. Every service in the mine compound strengthened her conviction that this would be a strategic crossroad of cultures that needed constant exposure to the gospel.

She wrote Wynn Stairs, missionary secretary of the United Pentecostal Church, outlining her dream of a church and day school for Bomi Hills village. The teacher and books could be provided for $30.00 a month. Authorities promised a grant of twelve acres for housing. By faith, she saw a church, school and home built where proliferate jungle and saw grass had reigned undisturbed for centuries. Best prospect of all, she could continue evangelizing in the rainy season.

There were long talks with Georgia who shared her burden to reach more villages, and understood her longing to establish new bulwarks for the Name of Jesus. Approval of the project would mean separate bases, however they determined to remain one in spirit and make time for fellowship, precious and necessary.

April 1st, a letter to her children, Dugans, Grapel Shelby and the Berean class.

A man at Bolah talked with me Tuesday morning about working for the Lord. We knelt to pray and he received the Holy Ghost—took off shouting and praising the Lord. By the time he circled the town twice a crowd gathered, so we had three services instead of two!

The Head of the Devil Bush Society here told me weeping that he wants to serve Jesus. Time will tell whether he will pay the price or not.

The Tulsa church is sending $5.00 a month for the ones who help me evangelize. That buys their food with a little left over for clothes. Jack asked this morning if he could send for a pair of long white pants. I suggested he get food first and see if there was money over for clothes. This afternoon your package came and in it was the white pants he needed—a perfect fit. We have a time finding clothes for these young men. I do want them to look decent when they go out to preach. We appreciate your help.

A big thanks to you, and Halleujah to Jesus for the hose. I needed them desperately, can't manage without them—wear 'em as long as they hang together.

I'll take these balloons to the children in Bolah. They'll be so excited—have never seen any, I'm sure. They always run to meet me when

I go. Last week, a little naked boy about six years old clung around my waist with hands and feet until we reached our house. His father is dead a year and his mother died a few weeks ago. A little girl named Sohtah always runs from me as though I was a leopard—barely missed a pot of boiling water trying to get away this week. Her uncle caught her and brought her to me kicking and screaming. I gave her a mint bubble that tamed her completely. She stayed close to me until I took my hair down. My hose and hair remain a source of wonder to old and young alike. An old Christian man said, "Jesus is wonderful to make hair like that."

Just one request—let me know how much tambourines cost, we need two badly. We have no musical instruments.

Marie made Gladys happy when she wrote that she was going to Tulsa for Carmen's graduation. Though she longed for more to give, Gladys could only ask headquarters to send Carmen a part of her allotment for a graduation gift.

Excerpt from a letter to her daughters, April 4th.

Someday I hope to have time to write without rushing. Big News! I have permission to start the school at Bomi Hills! I must act quickly before the rains get too heavy, however the legal angle may take a lot of time.

I want to build near the highway, close enough to a creek for water. Brother Stairs said use the metal roof from Beajah for the house.

We have good news from Sister Gruse, she may return to Liberia to help us. Everything is falling into place—there's a teacher in Monrovia who would like to teach at Bomi Hills.

More good news—the refrigerator is only a day away. They brought the door today. I won't be here long to enjoy its benefits, but, I don't mind, I'd rather be where I can do the most for the Lord.

The land-grant palaver was long and tedious extending from the Department of the Interior at Monrovia to the manager of the mine in Bomi Hills. Its sweep touched every Chief, sub-Chief and Headman in the area. Fortunately, she was able to get her walking shoes resoled—a crude, thick job that inspired the remark,

"If I can pick them up and set them down, they'll be the very thing for these rough paths—looks do not matter in the jungle!"

In between here and there, she took time to help Georgia with a mission palaver resulting in the dismissal of Jim.

Word from Brother Stairs was both elating and discouraging. Good news—he would personally provide the teacher support until a sponsor could be found. Bad tidings—mission funds were so low their allotments would come by installments and might be cut. They were reminded to pray earnestly for their daily bread.

Since the land palaver sent her to Monrovia several times, Gladys was grateful for the new road

Teacher Brown

completed to Klay—only seven hours walking to Maheh Mission! On one trip she arranged for Lajetta Smith, the teacher, to go home with her, ready to move to Bomi Hills whenever possible.

April 14th, excerpt from a letter to Marie;

Flash! The refrigerator is here! We are sitting on a 'high limb' sipping ice water, iced tea and eating jello. I'll miss it when I go, but my heart has already moved to Bomi. The Africans cannot understand this business of 'cooking ice' with kerosene.

A furniture maker of the home-made variety near the mine has made four dining room chairs for me—nice, only need a coat of varnish. I have a table left by the Pettys and am ordering a bedstead. Now, I wish I had brought my pretty set of dishes!

While Gladys took care of the Mission to give Georgia a week in Monrovia, word came that the old leper-lady had died at Bolah and she was buried the same day. She rejoiced she was spared long enough to hear and obey the Gospel.

Building plans dangled that week while she wearily cared for five small children with whooping cough. She suffered the worst aching homesickness for her children yet, triggered in part by anxiety over Carmen's future—where would she live and work?

Georgia brought letters from her family with pictures that delighted her. Another letter, not so pleasing said, "Pray that funds will come in for your monthly check." She commented to Marie,

I cannot see how these people who are 'at ease in Zion', doing nothing when so much needs to be done, are going to stay in Zion. Too many millions are going to hell without a chance, and too many doing exactly nothing to prevent it. I feel a sermon coming on "Sleepers in Zion", but you don't need it, so I'll refrain.

When the land-grant finally came through it was conditional on Gladys surveying the twelve acres. She noted their instruments were not the most modern; the mission boys twisted bark and wound it in large balls of rope, she 'smelled off' the yards. Two of the boys cut a trail through thick vegetation and saw grass wide and high enough to pass through.

The tropical sun beat down shimmering hot, she left them for a short rest in a cooler place. In her absence they angled off through the middle of the property instead of going around it, after that, she stayed on the job regardless of the heat. At last, the narrow path extended around twelve acres and rope-unwinding operation began. Robert was to stand still and hold the end. J.D. took the ball of rope ahead unwinding as he went. She was in the middle walking and pulling. They walked and walked and walked in the oppresive heat. She wondered why the rope remained slack, thought uneasily they might have more land than they could care for. She yelled back at Robert, he answered too close by. She dropped the rope and walked back to check. He was shuffling along with half closed eyes bringing the end with him! Go back to the starting point—

Eight men worked for several weeks with cutlasses

(long knives) hacking out vines and undergrowth. On the second round the trees were felled, then cut in smaller pieces and piled with the brush to burn. Then the whole acreage was cleaned and bonfires made again of all that failed to burn before. Next, they dug out rampant vine roots and stumps. She marked each man's 'cut' every morning to avoid time-consuming disputes. They started to work in April and ended in September.

Building began long before clearing was done. She knew nothing about building with mud, sticks, rattan and mats, but had to learn. Early in May, Lajetta and Nancy moved with Gladys to a small native hut near the building sites, for continual supervision of the work.

Every worker was assigned a certain number of 'sticks' (poles) to bring from the jungle for his daily task. String of prescribed lengths measured the bunches of bamboo brought from the swamps. Rattan, the native rope that grows in the bush was split after they collected it—this was used to tie everything together—no nails. Gladys found the workmen could not be left alone. She must continually either make peace or encourage them to keep moving.

She had to estimate how many bundles of palm leaves would be required to roof the school and porches, and decide how many inches around the bundle each man must bring. Often, a measuring string was lost creating more palaver! No previous experience helped her figure the amount of sand needed for the cement floor. She learned to make a mark on each man's box for the level of sand, brought laboriously from the river bed. And learned patience on a higher level waiting for cement to be found, and rain to stop.

May 16th, from a letter to Marie;

I came back to Maheh today because Reggie has been sick. Even so, she baked a fresh-grated coconut cake—we decided to call it my birthday cake. I've promised to come again on her birthday the 29th of this month.

We have moved Petty's old stove to Bomi. It heats fine, but the oven will have to be repaired before we can bake. There was also a painted white cabinet eight feet long we sawed in half to move—it will be a nice divider between the dining room and kitchen in my mud palace. The roof, doors and windows from Beajah will help cut costs. I'll be so thankful when we can move in.

I've borrowed Reggie's army cot for a bed in our temporary quarters.

The palaver I mentioned with Jim, he'd been slipping over to the girls' dorm talking to them through the window. We dismissed him but he's begged so hard to come back, we punished him and gave him another chance.

Well, driver ants came in the house to celebrate my birthday! The boys sprayed kerosene from floor to ceiling, so they decided to leave—those that were able!

May 24th she wrote Carmen

I hope you haven't worried about not hearing from me. Sending messengers to Monrovia is expensive and takes a boy out of school for four days—so we've cut trips to twice a month. I think of you many times a days and am always anxious to hear from you.

I'm fine, gain weight every time I'm around Reggie's refrigerator. We are only 2½-3 hours walk apart—near enough to help each other in case of sickness or palaver.

The work on the new house moves slowly. I watched monkeys playing in the treetops behind our property today. When they fight sounds like angry hogs. Do you think you would like our neighbors? The girls and I wish we were moved in near them instead of living in this noisy, dirty village. They call this Vietown because Vie people live here. Believe me, their noise is uglier than that of the monkeys.

My allotment has been cut, I'm thankful it happened after you finished high school, but still came at a bad time. I'm trying to help the workers, buy a little home-made furniture, evangelize and pay the men a pittance working on the new place. Well, the Lord knows and will provide. I'll be praying for your needs to be supplied, too, honey.

I've shown your picture to everyone here, they think it is beautiful! I hope you had one made in your graduation gown.

Gladys and Georgia agreed it was time for Jason to assume responsibility for the works near Maheh, including Kowadee. Jack assisted him some and held services in Bolah and Bugbay to free Gladys for the building palaver.

The new Mission's location was ideal—on the new highway, about a quarter of a mile from the Mine's Head Office. Bomi is a Gola word meaning stone or rock, and the hill they mined was almost solid iron ore. Living permanently in this section, she could minister to mine workers, save many hours walking and the nine months of day school a year would benefit the whole community. Lajetta started school in the town kitchen early in June, and already ABC's could be heard over the whole village.

A young man was saved in one of the early services at Bolah who took the Christian name, Paul. He and Jack were dependable helpers in services and on business errands.

June the seventh, there was temporary relief from building struggles and frustrations. Box 44 out did itself and overflowed with delicious blessings—each lady received eighteen letters! Since it was their first mail in two weeks, they didn't budge until every letter was read five or six times with contented chirrups reliving the happenings every writer reported. She started a letter to Carmen that night:

Dearest Little Girl,

I've never enjoyed mail so much! Eighteen letters! Of course the ones from you and Marie are my delight. I lived the Senior Banquet and outing with you.

You asked the meaning of 'palaver'—it's trouble or a problem, small or great. 'Humbug' means worry or bother. A man who has eleven children said, "this baby 'palaver' is too much 'humbug'."

Well, clothes for our workers 'humbugs' me too much! They barely manage food and soap on $5.00 a month. Civilization has come to the jungle and our workers are looking disgraceful compared to other men. Nashville girls send a lot of clothes for girls. The Dugans sent two pairs of pants—I keep hoping someone will send more used men's clothes. This is an urgent need.

After you and Marie give your tithes I hope you will always give love offerings to the missionary cause, it's the most neglected phase of the Lord's work. I don't mean always to Liberia. I'm sure there are other fields handicapped by lack of funds.

Bomi Hills, June 11th

Much has happened since I started this letter. Paul brought packages 'galore'!

You gave your mom a beautiful surprise! Your picture is so sweet and lifelike and words fail to describe how thrilled I am about the record. I did the three hour walk to the mission in two and a half hours to play it. It was too wonderful listening to you play and sing, and to hear Trusie sing again. It's a good thing I don't have a Victrola, I'd wear this record out in a hurry—can't get enough of listening.

I mentioned the workers lack of clothes in the beginning of this letter and before it's ready to mail, here are packages from Sister Sybil Kraus with many things badly needed! It seemed there's been a long drought, but God has opened the windows and dumped out parcels of blessings. I received nine! Grapel's welcome box of food, the bedspread from Marie and the lovely pictures of you and Marie, the tambourines, record and dry beans, besides used clothing to help in the work—I'm truly rich!

While I was at Maheh, I altered sixteen dresses for the big girls and made several baby dresses. The little ones had a high day with the button basket, spools of thread and bits of cloth.

Thanks again for everything. I'll write every chance I get.

Love and kisses,
Mother

Gladys realized the young men couldn't help but compare their measly $5.00 a month with the unheard of $30.00 to $50.00 monthly wages paid to civilized workers by the mine. That's the way packages helped, clothing meant more to them than money. Sybil sent plain and printed flour sacks that covered a lot of nakedness! The man building the school told Nancy he would continue to build regardless of small pay, for he hoped Mother would give them some clothes. Keeping faith, she gave his wife a dress and a play suit for their baby. The only problem, they were too proud of their new clothes to wear them—they may be torn, and there might not be anymore!

A student in San Antonia, Texas, Virgil Hughes assumed responsibility for the $30.00 a month school support for the first of May. His father "Pop" Hughes, missionary secretary in Parkersburg, West Virginia, read some of her letters to the church and raised $175.00. That gift came just in time to save the building program from a complete halt.

Gladys started a garden, set out rose bush cuttings and fruit tree slips among the tough roots and stumps of her new ground. The builders optimistically hoped to have the school-chapel and her house completed by the middle of July.

June 30th, Georgia and Gladys left the teachers in charge and went to Monrovia together for their June support.

Brief letter to her family July 3rd.

A hurried note before we leave for the Interior. I'm so thankful for the twelve gauge shotgun Orlan sent me. It will mean meat for the table ***and*** *protection. The Lord has helped me, I'm not as scared as I used to be. Reggie is very nervous since she was sick—had a nightmare before the lights went out last night. Said she'll be glad to get back to the jungle where it's safe!*

I bought roofing we lacked and paint for doors and shutters—hope there's enough for interior matting.

I have small gifts to send later,

Love and Kisses

Gladys bought $14.00 half share of chickens at Maheh but the hawks zeroed in on the flock and there was not enough left to divide. She hoped someday the scrawny, tough chickens of the tropics with their tiny eggs would be replaced by a better strain and welcomed a sturdier gift—two ducks. They waddled over the new ground faring sumptiously on bugs and worms.

"Nancy! Come look!" she called excitedly one morning, "A duck is laying—here's a nest with four eggs. If she'll 'agree' to set when there's a few more eggs, won't that be good!"

Reggie made her first visit to Bomi and spent the day with her. They celebrated with the firstfruits of the garden—tender green beans. Gladys thought they had all gone for bug fare, as the okra did.

July 25th Gladys wrote Carmen:

In answer to your questions about my house. Buildings here are framed by standing slender poles, (they call them sticks) tied with split strips of rattan. Small limbs are woven here and there through the poles, and the whole affair daubed with mud until the walls are from twelve to eighteen inches thick. They will soon be ready to start daubing my house.

Ants process ground to make it waterproof, so their hills are broken down, crushed fine and used for the mud mix. We moved six large ones from the three acres we've cleared, so there's plenty, but I'll have to encourage them to daub enough on. After the mud is on,the women rub the walls until they are as smooth as plaster (more or less!).

There's white clay on the creek bottoms that is almost like white paint. Some of the natives rub it on their walls, then paint designs on them with other colors of clay.

I want my walls rubbed with white clay, and have light blue paint for wood doors and shutters. I hope we can paint the metal roof red, have ivory color for ceilings, inside walls and mats.

It will take eight bags of cement for my floor—have only been able to get two. If I can carry out all of my plans, my house will look nice, and be cool and comfortable.

I'm happy and busy here, but I look forward to the day when I'll step off a plane or a train and hug you hard and we'll have a long, long time together. Maybe we'll meet in the rapture, so stay ready, Dear, in case Jesus hastens His coming.

Until we meet again, I know He will take care of you for me.

All my love,

Shortage of funds hampered the work, however, July's allotment was enough to relieve the strain, she rejoiced, "The Lord knew my need and provided!"

More halleujah news! Brother Williams raised $250.00 at a District Conference for her a refrigerator. Sister Gruse would bring it when she sailed out of New Orleans November the first, on her way back to Liberia. Sybil wrote, 'five packages are on the way, Sisters Graham and King packed them, and Frank Muncie paid the postage.'

August 9th, from a letter to Marie and her husband Glenn.

You can see I'm using the paper you sent. I'm saving the chocolate syrup for the long trips, when building is finished. No work going on today for African rain is pouring down, down, down.

One year ago I landed in Africa for the first time at Dakar. What a year it's been!

Ruthie's mother is staying with her sister at Vietown so I can help her when her baby is born. Looks like it could happen anytime, and I know nothing about playing midwife!

Did I tell you the duck 'agreed' and is sitting on eleven eggs! I must give her the credit, there would have been twelve, but I ate one!

Fahmah has nearly finished the mats for the house. I finally learned his name is actually 'Farmer', but these folks don't sound the letter 'r'—so I say Fahmah, too.

Extra money made it possible to hire three more men for clearing the ground, but they are hindered by frequent rain.

I'm sending my broken glasses, please have repaired and return—have headaches when I read without them.

The school transferred from the town kitchen to the new school building the last week of August. Torrential rain washed away a vital bridge, however school children crossed the river on a makeshift bridge by holding to a rattan rope.

Supervising the workmen kept Gladys so rigidly

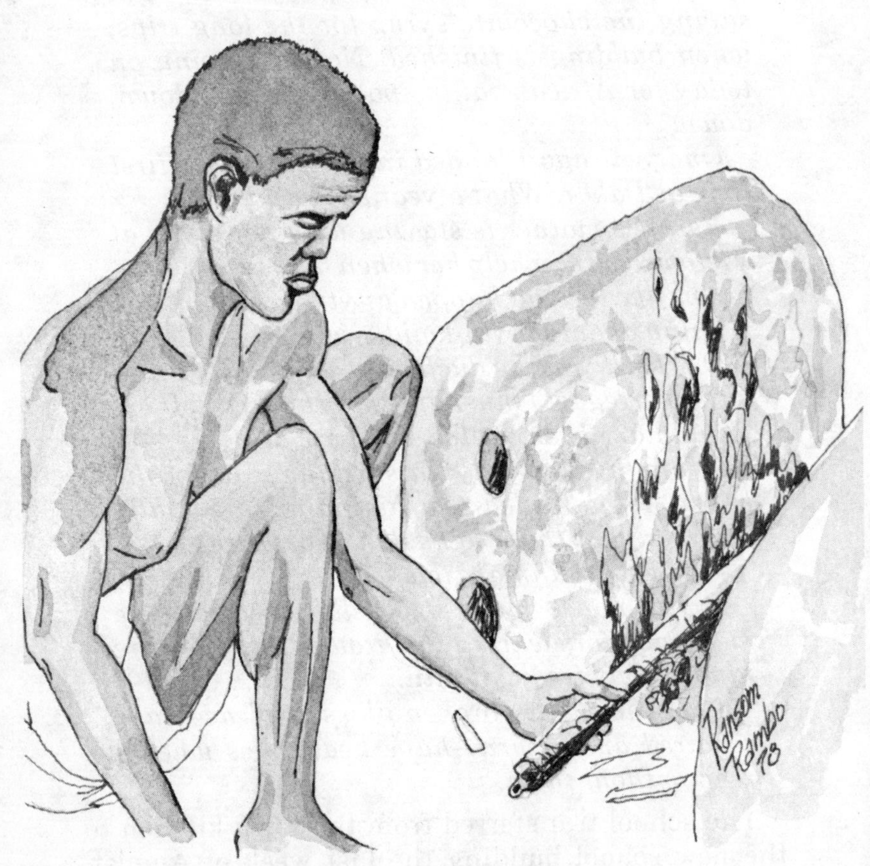

Worker and smelter (The ancient way.)

on the job, there wasn't much time for letter writing. Three stumps in front of her house were removed with slow tedium. She waited months for the home she hoped to occupy in a few weeks when the project began in April.

August 25th, letter to Carmen

I appreciated hearing about the camp meeting—know you were glad to see Trusie and Wayne Rooks again. I've received a letter from John Paul Hughes, (brother of Virgil) asking about missionary work in Africa. I wrote him concerning needs in Dakar and Liberia. I hope he has a call.

Tell me when you hear more about the plane missing from Dakar. I'm not surprised if it's like the "jalopy" I flew down here. It even leaked!

Moses is still at Maheh. His latest bright remark was "I'm hungry for the Gospel." I told Reggie we might as well lay down our cross and go home, if in spite of all our efforts the mission children are starving for the Gospel.

Did you get my request for jar lids and rubber rings? We need them as soon as possible because the calf is eating everything green on the mission.

Reggie visited me yesterday, I've been staying on the job and haven't been to Maheh for quite awhile.

I'm "jammed" for time, a messenger is waiting for me to finish this letter, but if I wrote all day I couldn't tell you how much I love you.

Gladys took advantage of a few sunny days to take an expedition with the teacher and school children to Beajah mission for flowers and trees to plant at Bomi. They waded or were carried over several streams. Virgil Hughes, a small boy named for the school's sponsor, slipped on a log crossing a creek and fell in with a loud splash. The teacher's shoes he carried was lost, but older boys dived until they found them. Virgil was never in danger for he swam like a fish.

She decided the returning procession resembled Israel on the wilderness journey, everyone carrying his load, holding it high when they walked through water. They brought back a bushel each of limes and grapefruit, and many shrubs and small trees for planting. Paul helped her border the paths with hibiscus, a shrub with large brilliant-red flowers.

Services in the spacious new school made a glad contrast to the cramped, drab town kitchen. The builders so often made unrealistic predictions on the completion of her house, she did not believe when they said 'the tenth of September--definitely!'

Letter, September the 14th:

Dear children, All Three of You!

I've marked off the workman's tasks, taught Bible class at school, next on my list is letters.

Fahman's wife is putting white clay on the chapel-school—looks better. We have a big Liberian flag and some large pictures at the front. If we had good benches it would look nice. I hope to have some made of rough planks before long for the bug-a-bugs are eating the bamboo benches.

The carpenter says our house may be finished this week. Nancy Ann said, "the day we move to that house, is the day we move to heaven." We have spent five months in this leaky hut with rats in the thatch roof continually knocking trash down on us, and keeping us awake with their noise. There was a new leak right in my face last night, but the umbrella and rain coat were in use elsewhere. Nancy and the teacher complained with me about the rain dripping on us all night until we remembered that Jesus had no place to lay His head—not even a leaky hut!

We have so much to be thankful for—it's the 'hungry' time, now. Rice, the daily bread is scarce. We have enough to last another month, when the new rice will be harvested—hard to hold on to it with many hungry mouths around us. So many strangers have moved into this area, there is a cassava shortage, too and prices are exorbitant whenever there is food for sale.

However, the saddest lack in Africa is the 'Bread of Life.' Services were blessed Sunday. I preached on the Blood both morning and evening. What a joy to tell them about the Lamb of God—but, having to pause for three interpreters does hinder the anointing. We have twelve different tribes represented in our school, including two from the Gold Coast.

THANKS for my glasses. I needed them. I've stood over the carpenters all day today. Fahmah has decided since he works for the mission, a man "of his standing" should have a pair of shoes. Well, I've decided that a person of "my standing" should have curtains and couch cover to match, since that will be my sole furnishing for the living room. You are wondering where I'll get the couch? We are going to try make one of rough planks and rattan, then dress it up. I'll fill pillows with dry palm thatch. I'm sending some marked pictures from the catalog and two twenty dollar bills, you girls decide what will be best considering "my standing" back here in the jungles!

We'll be moving in when the floors are dry, maybe by the time you get this letter, though we are running low on cement, my bedroom is done.

They say the road will soon join this side of Klay, if true, my next trip to Monrovia will be easier—I plan to go the 29th, either Reggie or me need to be there every month to cash our checks. I want to see the Syrian dentist about my upper plate. They fit badly—too loose. If they fly out while I'm preaching sometime I'm sure my audience would think they are being 'witched' and run away. Most of them have never seen false teeth. I lost them one night praying with the seekers in the altar service but, don't think anyone knew what happened! Events happened thick and fast the last half of September.

16th—A two-headed snake came out of the thatch roof over the large back porch.

17th— The second one stuck his double head out, so loose thatch was removed and replaced by cord thatch, more compact, made by twisting or plaiting the palm leaves.

18th— The carpenters completed the wood work.

19th— Pouring cement floors came to a halt four bags short of completion.

20th— Jack started the tedious task of painting the interior mats.

21st— Mary Ruth's plump baby brother arrived in the early morning. Hard rain prevented the old cronies taking the mother to the creek for delivery as usual. Precious time had to be divided to teach baby-care.

22nd— Vain attempt to get cement.

23rd— Same! they started rubbing walls with white clay.

24th— RED LETTER DAY. Gladys, Nancy and Lajetta moved into her bedroom—at last!

25th— Glorious news by way of the Pentecostal Herald—Brother Box appealed for funds to buy a truck for Liberia. She could hardly believe what she read.

26th— Went to Maheh to rejoice with Reggie over truck prospect and move some of her things to Bomi.

27th— She had to get a permit from the Mine Head office to travel on the new road.

28th— Gladys and Jack got on a truck and rode all the way from the Mine to Monrovia with a short wait at Klay! Preview of better days to come. The road was completed except for some minor bridges and fill.

30th—The day started early organizing helpers to assist Jack taking their loads (including cement!) up the river to Mittsburg where carriers waited. Only mine personnel and mine freight was allowed on the new road, with the exception of missionaries and their aids.

Gladys wrote letters and did what everyone in Africa does, sooner or later—waited. She felt she could ill afford $2.25 a day for board. If she left Monrovia before their checks came, two more trips would have to be financed; send a messenger for the mail, bring the checks to the mission for their signature, and take them back to Monrovia to be cashed. Hours and hours of walking and much expense involved. Her pictures were a disappointment—the film molded in the camera. Dental work was out of the question, too expensive.

A stack of packages were heartening, pretty oil cloth and utensils for her kitchen, magazines and food from Marie, clothes and food from Lunelle and Grapel.

The checks came October the third and early the next morning she was on the road home, thankful the trip could be made in less than half a day on the new road, even with two or three stops.

She wrote her children October 12th.

Here I sit at Maheh mission as though I didn't have a thing in the world to do. Ruth is tucked up in my lap, so cute with her tiny braids. I can hardly write, she won't 'agree' to get down. She 'humbugs so plenty'!

While I was in Monrovia her baby brother, John David, was very sick. The teacher and Nancy advised the parents to bring him to Reggie. Last Saturday she sent word he was worse, his parents came over with me. Thank the Lord, he's better today, and if he keeps improving he'll take him back to Bomi tomorrow. We keep telling them no one can 'witch' this baby since they are converted. Statistics have shown only two out of every ten babies live. It's sad.

I'm still waiting for the cement to be brought from Paul's River so the floors can be finished.

When I mailed your monkey skins from Monrovia, I wished for $20.00 to buy the huge leopard skin for you I saw there.

Please thank the P.M.C. for the offering they sent. It made some extras possible I needed. I'm happy for all the things you've sent lately. I really am ashamed I haven't written more, but there has been no time.

I'll be so glad when this building "palaver is finish" so I can do missionary work again. It takes different kinds of work to spread the Gospel, and though building at Bomi Hills is a direct blessing from God, yet evangelism is urgently needed. We expect to hit the jungle trail again in two or three weeks, Halleujah!

I dreamed of being home a few nights ago but you girls were asleep, I thought I would wait until morning to see you, and the next thing I was in Africa and far away. I keep wishing I had wakened you so I could, at least, have enjoyed you in my dreams.

Box 44 was a hollow disappointment for over three weeks except for a cable that said her refrigerator was on the way to Africa.

Two more blessings; John David recovered fully and contributed baby-brightness to grace weary days, and carriers brought the cement from Paul's River to finish the mission house floors.

October, 25th
Hello Girls!

Would you like to drop in and see my jungle home?

I made curtains for the kitchen windows out of the blue material with red apples (I bought in Tulsa for a housecoat) trimmed them with a ruffle of red oilcloth. The work table and shelves are covered with red and the linoleum is black, gray and red.

The dining room end of the long room has my new set of pink dishes on the sideboard. My old red table cloth is on the table with a pink bowl full of oranges. I didn't have a choice of color for the floor covering—it's wine.

The woven grass plaid rug for the living room area is tan and blue, ten by twenty feet. The cheap day bed and mattress I bought in Monrovia waits for its cover to make it a couch. I found a long narrow table at Beajah and refinished it to hold books. All my family smiled at me from the card table I bought from Reggie.

For my bedroom, I made one of my famous dressing tables flounced with the pink-flowered material Sybil sent. The pretty red ribbon from Nashville was probably meant for hair ribbon, but it makes a beautiful bow at the front of the table. My mirror hangs over it. How I appreciate my bed after five months sleeping on an army cot! Floor to ceiling white net is positioned to tuck under the mattress at night so I can sleep in peace. There was enough of the oil cloth for the bathroom shelves and room there to hang my clothes.

My bedroom opens on the back porch where we gather for prayer morning and evening. It has thatched roof, dirt floor, mud bannisters and is usually cool. I have a hammock there. Bright red hibiscus bloom in the front of the house. It looks homelike, and we are winding up the building palaver, praise the Lord, so we can go on Gospel trips again—all of us are glad.

The natives are harvesting rice and working hard to keep rice birds driven from the fields. A 'mob' of birds built a bird village in some mission tree tops. Nearby farmers wanted to top the trees to get rid of them, and I agreed. The nests are made of palm thatch strips partially covered. I hung one by the front door. A school girl picked up a baby bird, we put it in the nest, and now, he yells for rice whenever anyone passes by!

Jack is painting the metal roof red, Robert and the workmen have gone to the creek for more white clay to finish rubbing the house.

We all went to the camp last night for service, there was a large crowd and good interest. A drunk man disturbed the beginning, but native style, they beat him and put him to bed—no more palaver.

I tried again to make pictures of the mission but my film is molded and stuck together. My lamp is nearly out of oil and getting dim so must stop.

Lots of love, Mother

Chapter 11
BACKWARD AND FORWARD

November 1st

Dear Missionary Club,

You will never know how your letters and packages have blessed me. I especially appreciate reports on the services there and rejoice with you in the blessings of God.

I feel like I've been wandering in a desert for the past six months while we were building instead of evangelizing. We've had our "porch service" morning and evening and meetings in the mine camp, but we have missed reaching the villages with the message they desperately need. We are seeing some fruit from the school—three of the largest boys received the Holy Ghost this week.

Sunday nights, the meetings are held in a large opening in the middle of the camp and the people stand patiently all through the service. Last night I told them exactly where all drunkards and gamblers are going according to God's

Word. Almost every man in the camp falls in that category. Our audiences change every few months with new ones coming in and others transferred away—this effort can have far-reaching effects.

We found driver ants had invaded the mission when we returned from church. They were all around the porch and kitchen, the boys drove them away with burning bamboo torches.

When we were granted this twelve-acre-tract of ground, I thought it would take about six weeks to get the clearing done and the buildings erected—how wrong I was! The work was divided into three contracts, I didn't expect to supervise every inch either, but soon found it was necessary. I trusted the carpenters, so some of the inside walls look like a tornado struck them in places, but the natives look at paint on the inside walls and carpets on the floors and say, "fine past anything we've seen!"

Do you understand why you haven't heard from me for six months? I hope you'll forgive me for not writing. I will have more time now, and certainly have better living conditions. The only light in the native hut was a small kerosene lantern and the roof leaked so much when it rained, we couldn't burn it!

As I close this I see a schoolgirl in a Nashville dress running and jumping. I wish I had a movie of her to send you. I don't have to remind these youngsters to pray for those who have clothed them. I hardly have the nerve to ask you to keep the letters coming, but, I hope you do!

Your co-worker for Jesus,

Gladys Robinson

p.s. The enclosed dried flower is a coffee bloom. They have many flowerlets on a spike with unusually sweet fragrance. Coffee is grown commercially here, but I haven't seen the natives drink it. Until they are converted they prefer sugar cane gin and palm wine!

A messenger came from Maheh with unhappy news. The fatted calf simply lay down and died. Goodbye to their hopes of steak, roasts and hamburgers! He brought other information so sad the demise of a mere calf paled into insignificance. They faced a serious palaver when Georgia returned from Monrovia where she waited for their October checks.

November 15th, letter to Carmen;

Two letters from you last week! And the newspaper that came in a week. Imagine seeing a newspaper only a week old back here in the jungle!

Our school closed last Friday morning. When our "stir off" was over, Jack, Nancy, Paul and John David went with me to Maheh for their closing program Friday night. Had court all day Saturday and returned to Bomi Sunday morning.

One we trusted fell into sin—such a disappointment.

We struggled to cross the long swamp on the way to Bolah last week. I took off my steamed-up glasses while trying to balance. Paul put them in his pocket. He made the poles secure enough to walk on then hunted new ones to add to the walkway. We finally got across, went through another town, crossed a big creek on a log and were near Bolah when Paul discovered my glasses were missing. He went back to look for them and met Robert, our workman, who had decided on the spur of the moment, to go home for the night. While crossing the swamp, he miraculously spotted the glasses in a clear spot of water about a foot deep, and was bringing them to me!

I lost them once before on the way to Kowadee—they lay for one week right where I stepped off the log into the path. Many people passed that way every day, but they were not broken when they were found. The natives say God takes care of my glasses for me, but I think I'll keep them on in the future, steam or no steam!

Have I told you what 'hardhead' means! Its noise, especially persistent asking or crying. Well, John David is making big 'hardhead' for chop—he say 'stomach not full plentee' and the nice bird is making 'hardhead' for his chop too! Too much Palaver!

Later—things have quietened down 'small-small', so I'll go on with my letter. I tried again, to get pictures of my house, but more molded film prevented.

A note from Reggie, she plans to bring Gladys and the babies and spend a few days with me. It's true, we don't get to visit each other often, but really enjoy whenever it happens.

There has been so much strenuous work on hand, I've put off fasting, but recently the Lord spoke to me so plainly, "when are you going to fast?" I started the next day. I'm convinced Apostolic power will only come by prayer and fasting.

Be sweet, and write, I miss you and Marie so much—often call Nancy, 'Marie' or 'Carmen'.

Lots of Love

John David's 'hardhead' made her realize his mother Vinnah needed to learn how to care for him. She said,

"He's sweet and cute, but I can't afford to be tied down, even by a cute little thread like him."

Vinnah's husband Birmah was mission guard with responsibilities that increased when Gladys made trips. She asked them to build a home on the mission so Birmah could take care of things more efficiently.

Gladys mailed the meager Christmas gifts she managed to get for her girls—a book each and a small leopard skin which she suggested they divide and use for trimming a coat.

November 23rd
Dear Children,

I'm at Maheh Mission again. More palaver, heartaches and disappointment. Satan has

trapped young workers and struck a vital blow against our plans for evangelism, this time. A giant step backward.

Then yesterday, I received the greatest disappointment since I came to Liberia, with a letter saying the missionary prayer meetings were discontinued. I wonder if someone decided we didn't need prayer anymore? The news came just when we needed prayer support the most!

Reggie spent a day and night with me last week. We visited the four Dutch families who live near. It's nice having them here, though we don't have a lot in common. Mrs. Buekin is older and we communicate better with her. She and her husband were in concentration camps in Java during the war.

I read the article on Liberia in the October Digest. It was a good description, but the writer must not have gone far into the Interior because, occasionally we do find a bush back here that doesn't have opportunities hanging in it. He described Monrovia fairly accurately. The next few years will probably bring many changes and Liberia needs them.

Nancy and I planned to go home tomorrow, but since it's Thanksgiving Reggie insists we must spend another day and have chicken and dressing and ice cream. She never wants me to leave when I come and I'm the same way about her when she visits me.

So many letters to write, I'll sign off, now.

Love and kisses

Nancy took a boat home from Monrovia when word came her mother was critically ill in Los Palmos. Gladys felt as though her hands were cut off—did not realize before how much she depended on Nancy.

The need of fellowship took her to Maheh again, December the first. Amusing baby-talk, and the comical antics of Joanna and Mary Ruth were a soothing balm. Naomi took two jiggers out of her toes. Joanna with a hairpin pretended she was removing jiggers, too!

Gladys confided her frustration.

"Reggie, there's two things, like dead weights, holding me down when I'm really anointed to preach. One is waiting for three interpreters and the other is my teeth. Maybe it's good I have to wait for the interpreters, for after every sentence I have to get a new grip on my upper plate. Since these folks know nothing of dentures, if they fly out of my mouth, they'd probably expect my hands and feet to fly off next!"

December 11, 1948
Dear Children,

I came to Monrovia last Monday with a long list of things to do.

I was at the War Department working on permits for Sister Gruse's guns when a message reached me, Joanna died suddenly Tuesday night, the 7th.

Reggie took her to Suehn Mission for treatment, she died there a few hours later. The Baptist Missionary sent me to Suehn with his truck. The box to bury her in was finished so late, we held her funeral in the chapel at sundown and buried her in Suehn's graveyard after dark. If she wasn't in Suehn I would have missed the funeral for it isn't possible to keep a body long here. The missionaries at Suehn were kind and thoughtful—couldn't have done more.

Reggie is broken hearted. You can't imagine how sweet the babies are and how much they mean to us. It's so refreshing to pick one of them up and forget palavers for a while. Joanna was the sunshine of Maheh Mission. To think, the pictures we took the last day I was there didn't turn out—the film was bad. She wasn't well that day, but, we didn't dream it was anything serious.

I had to return to Monrovia because of unfinished business. Reggie felt she couldn't go home alone, so came to Monrovia with me. Suehn's truck took us to Millsburg. We came on the river boat from there. The tide was out, and we were stuck on a sandbar for three hours, a quarter of a mile from Monrovia! Both of us were sick with headaches from emotional pressure and the heat, but a night of rest helped and we feel better today.

I could write on and on, but we are trying to get a way on the new Highway this morning. We need to get back to Maheh. They say the girls are grief-stricken. I'll spend a few days with them before I go home.

The couch cover and curtains came—only had

time to peek, but looks lovely. A gift of $63.00 from the Mission Club saved the day for me—would have been short without it. The food box they sent looks so good. Say "many thanks", I'll write them later.

I received another letter from John Paul Hughes, he is really interested in Africa.

Must hurry—love and kisses,

Leaving Monrovia at noon Saturday made them miss a ride from Klay to Maheh Crossing. They spent the night with Dutch friends and learned the mine was now issuing permits for trucks and jeeps to travel the new road to Bomi. If Gladys was going home she could have ridden to her door, instead, she walked twelve miles with Georgia to Maheh.

Maheh Mission
December 15th
Dear Children,

I wonder if this letter will reach you by Christmas! This hot weather, the same humid-hot every day makes it hard to realize its Christmas time again. We hoped Sister Gruse would be with us, but haven't heard anything yet.

We cooked the black-eyed peas you girls sent and you wouldn't believe how quickly they vanished from our plates! Still our "stummicks are not full plentee" of those delicious things. And the cheese! We have just eaten dried apple pie with slices of cheese.

Box 44, Monrovia

Ten hours later,

Reggie has a government surveyor here surveying five hundred acres for the mission. He is a old man, father of the Vice-President of Liberia, and he brought several aides with him. The Clan Chief had to be here in his robes to witness the cutting of the line (with two helpers). The whole place was in a stew all day. We cooked three meals and waited on them hand and foot. When they all finally went to the new house to sleep, we hoped for peace and quiet, but I picked Ruth up and discovered she was hot with fever, over 103 degrees. We examined her throat and there were white spots on her tonsils. We didn't want to believe Joanna had diptheria but the evidence points that way. If so, all the little ones here and at Suehn have been exposed. I'll finish this letter in the morning.

December 17th

I'm too rushed and upset to write much. We are sending Robert to Monrovia to notify Health authorities we have diptheria here. We are concerned about Ruth, but don't worry about us, this is a child's disease.

I dreamed both of you girls came to see me last night and I kissed you—so real and sweet. Have a good Christmas!

Love and kisses, Mother

December 20th, Bomi Hills

Darling Babies of mine,

This is a short note to say I love you a lot, and I

never get too busy to think of you and long for you. I wish I could have contributed more toward making your Christmas happy.

God has heard our prayers—Ruth is better! Reggie sends love.

Food poisoning on the twenty-second of December didn't encourage their appetites for Christmas dinner at Maheh on the twenty-fourth. Poison ivy made Georgia uncomfortable, and the old familiar specter of homesickness sat close to both ladies—always more acute at Christmas. They bravely tried to be jolly, singing carols and giving gifts on Christmas Eve, to the mission family at Maheh.

Early Christmas morning Gladys hurried back to Bomi to prepare for the Christmas palaver there. The new house was festive! Palm thatched stuffed pillows and the new cover made the day bed a couch, its' giant pink daisy print matched the living room curtains. Her bed wore the new spread sent by Marie, and youngsters brought in beautiful flowers from the jungle—branches of golden yellow balls and deep red spirals of blooms.

Many of the parents who came were Moslems. It was their first time to attend a Christian service. Gladys took ample time for the message that was translated into Gola, Mendy and Vie were pleased with the response.

Thanks to loving folks in America there were gifts, novelties, clothes and refreshment for all who came—their gratitude sweetened the missionary's loneliness.

The day after Christmas was a day of tidings.

Sister Gruse and the refrigerator were waiting in Monrovia for a guide and transport, Box 44 had a collection of package notices, and three more babies were sick at Maheh.

December 29th, Monrovia
My Family,

I came on Monday—got a truck in front of my door and rode all the way to Monrovia! Sister Gruse is fine, I'm so glad she is here. We need her badly.

She brought me a large mirror I need and the film I requested. The merchant came down on the price, so Pauline and I both bought a victrola. You've heard about an old hen and one chicken? I have a victrola and one record. I'm afraid I'll soon wear out the one you sent for my birthday, Carmen.

I have a bounty of packages, the Christmas box from you, Glenn and Marie. (Can't hardly wait to get in it!), and four from Freda and Grapel. Margaret Stairs and a church in California sent each of us a welcome box of linens and food.

It's thrilling to know my refrigerator is here. I don't think it will take as long to get it home as Reggie waited for hers.

I started this letter in the room and am finishing it at the Post Office.

Love and kisses, plenty!

Here is a letter from Nancy Ann, mission girl, to the Sunday School class in Nashville that sponsored her.

Maheh Mission school
January 10, 1949

Dearest Friends,

I am greeting you all in our wonderful Saviour Name. Thanks to the Lord for what you doing for me. All the clothes you send us, we get them with happiness.

When I kneel down in my prayer, I remember you all. I well glad you have the thought of we dark West Africa children, more than our own parents can do.

Mother Robinson tell me how well you love Jesus, and nice to everyone, and how that class work for the Lord.

Mother love children, she loves me. She always go out for evangelize. When she go out she must carry us with her to tell our people about Jesus. Our people sin too much. Ma Robinson had two places she preach and other places she preach too. The people believe in Jesus now, we going around trips to teach them.

May please pray for us that we can win plenty souls. I am glad I know Jesus now. He speak in my heart.

I close with my love to all.

Your Christian girl,
Nancy Ann

1949
February 8th, Bomi Hills
Dear Children,

Seems I always write in a hurry. I've been

behind with letters since before Christmas—Joanna's death, having to be at Maheh so much, palavers, trips to Monrovia, besides the merry-go-round here at home. I've been doing the cooking—a complicated job—water has to be boiled and filtered, then the filter cleaned every day. Nancy hasn't returned and since I couldn't keep up, I hired a cook. He's of the Bussi tribe, wanted me to give him a Christian name. I call him Glenn after my son-in-law. I've arranged for his schooling and give him $5.00 a month. He's quiet and tries hard to please.

FLASH! The refrigerator is here! Perfectly wonderful! I had a fright when we brought it up. A crew of six held it upright on a top-heavy canoe across the St. Paul river. One was drunk, one naked and all of them careless. I watched horrified from the bank as the boat rocked violently. I turned away to keep from seeing it go down, then went behind the bushes and walked up and down the bank and prayed. God answered my cry!

This refrigerator furnished ice for the President of Liberia when he visited Bomi Hills last week. Mrs. Buekin had eight 'big' men from New York, I contributed ice to her hospitality, and send one or other of the Dutch families ice everyday since they transport so much for us.

Brother Stairs wrote Reggie that three years is long enough in the tropics and she must go home at the end of this year. The Public Health examiner in Monrovia said the same thing. She is taking treatment for parasites while she spends two weeks vacation with me.

God bless Pauline! Her coming was exactly the right time—hardly a chance to catch her breath before she took over Maheh to give Reggie a break.

Gladys shared every interesting event with her children but failed to mention her deteriorating health. Georgia and Pauline saw what she tried to hide, nevous tension and chronic fatigue, and wondered how she kept going.

February 15th, Bomi Hills
Dear Rea and Glen,

I have a circular letter and stacks of others ready to go. The circular gives full details but must tell you that two received the Holy Ghost Sunday night at the Mission.

On the ninth of January, after church the tailor came running to say his wife "deliver." She is Vinnah's sister, this is her tenth baby, all of them starved to death—the ninth one died about a year ago (the one Vinnah brought to Maheh).

Just as I entered the hut where she lay on a mat of thin bamboo strips, they put the baby in steaming hot water, it yelled and so did I. It ended by me bringing him to the Mission to bathe him—just what they wanted, of course.

Vinnah is doing so well with John David, I put this baby in her care. The tailor has work now, and is able to buy the milk, he's over a month old and doing fine. They think he's safe from witches on the Mission ground.

Birmah and Vinnah are a blessing taking care of the Mission when I'm away. She is neat and intelligent with remarkable faith. There was a dangerous job to be done, I hesitated to ask Birmah. Vinnah said, "Birmah pray God, then He can do it."

Reggie is still with me, I'll miss her when she leaves, but there's no chance for loneliness—always something happening.

I have a lot of visitors, so thankful to have a place for travelers to stay. I expect the Richardsons today, may stop a couple of nights. I'm cooking some of the butter beans you sent, frozen deer meat, and I'll make ice cream. Imagine ice cream in the jungles!

The temporary chapel-school building was inadequate for the church crowds and beyond repair, side mats brought from Beajah sagged with rotteness. She decided to use her Christmas offering for a new building, hoping $50.00 would complete it. Other buildings were needed and planned, waiting for God's provision.

The bamboo benches weakened by bug-a-bugs frequently spilled their occupants. Whenever possible she bought planks to build sturdier benches—eight were completed.

March 1st, Monrovia

Just a line, Reggie and I both have several things to see about. Brother Stairs is sending us a truck on faith and credit, may be here next month—isn't that wonderful!

The baby Vinnah took care of became seriously ill on the 21st. I thought I couldn't bear to see the mother lose her tenth baby, so Reggie and I joined in begging God to spare him. It seemed the Lord put us to sleep the 24th and took him. His father is Moslem but wanted a Christian funeral. The carpenter made a box, we lined it with white and had masses of flowers. Pauline came with some of the children from Maheh and she brought the message. It was the first Christian funeral ever held in this area.

I decided to have a check up while at the U.S. public Health Mission. Verdict; no fever, worms or parasites, but dangerously overworked. The Doctor gave me a choice, two weeks absolute rest, or go home within six months, with a total collapse. I know God is able, but I can't get around Reggie and Pauline's arguments any longer. They've been worried about me for sometime and have begged me to rest.

How can I rest? I can turn the Mission over to Joseph—he's trustworthy—and the teacher can handle the school, but I'm haunted day and night by the villages. People are begging for the Gospel and dying daily. It seems so heartless to stretch out and relax in the face of such need. I don't understand why no one volunteers to come and help. I guess I'll have to comply in order to stay here. It won't be easy.

I'm so thankful you are meeting at the church to pray for us—now, you understand how much it's needed.

Gladys rested at Maheh for three weeks, Rachel and Naomi spent the nights with her in what was still called the "new house." It was very quiet, Reggie or Pauline came by occasionally for a few minutes. Vinnah brought John David to see her because he cried so much after she left.

"Vinnah, you shouldn't have carried that fat baby over here", she said. "And don't worry about me. I expect to live a long time in this world and forever in the next one!"

Her glasses slipped out from under 'protection' and broke on the cement floor. She sent the remains to Marie with a please rush back." She wanted to keep writing, at least to her family, but the slightest effort left her tembling in weakness.

Since there was no improvement and she longed continually for her room at Bomi, Pauline offered to go with her and assume responsibility of the Mission until she recovered.

Letters became abbreviated small notes to her family imploring them to pray and not worry.

March 29th

So thrilled to get home. Pauline has moved her things over, seems as concerned with the Mission and the villages as I am. She is certainly fine.

Reggie leaves on furlough in a few months and I may have to come home early. Is there no one willing to fill the yawning gaps made by our leaving?

Do not worry, this is not a serious illness—I'm just exhausted and nervous. Pray!

April 3rd

That was quick service! How I appreciate my glasses after doing without them for a while. They came yesterday.

A large group of Bolah converts came for service this morning and to see me. Even the old, old man who said we were a lamp in their darkness tottered in. They brought two chickens and some eggs.

Pauline has started a garage for the truck. She has great hopes for Bomi Hills as a training center for Gospel workers. I certainly love her.

April 9th

Tell all "hello" and please keep praying, though I'm not improving, prayers is keeping me as well as I am.

Sister Sybil sent orders for me to go to Monrovia for a six weeks' rest, but there's no resting place there—too much chaos and noise.

April 16th

Brother Stairs recommends three months rest in Monrovia. All of you please pray, I could bear laying around for three more months if I thought it would put me back on the job. Now, don't worry, I'm not ill—just tired.

Mother Holmes is here for a few days rest, she is worn out—over fifty-three years in the jungle.

April 19th

I was able to enjoy some of the services during the Fellowship Meeting. Forgot I was sick when the Bugbay Chief came through speaking in tongues! Many filled.

I'm able to stay out of bed more, less nervous, and getting stronger, so you can stop worrying. The Board says three more months rest, but that seems too long a sentence.

I can't keep up with correspondence, feel the effects when I try to write, but we are faring sumptiously through the generosity of God's children.

May 6th

Pauline and I came to Monrovia this week. The doctor agrees I'm better off in the Interior unless he can find something that requires treatment.

I hope it's God's will I stay in Liberia, however I'm useless without my health.

May 9th

We return to Bomi Hills tomorrow with the doctor's approval. I hope Sybil and the others will understand. They don't know Monrovia—I'd as soon be in jail, have felt worse since we came.

The doctor thinks I should come home for a few months. I'd hate to leave when I'm needed so badly here—though I'm no good as I am. I'm leaving it up to the Lord and our leaders.

Someone's prayers have brought me safely through a little round of malaria.

May 23rd

No news, nothing strange or exciting, except

the toad-size grasshopper that got up Pauline's dress a few nights ago and broke up the prayer meeting.

I'd be ashamed to come home 'sick' as fat as I am. I sit here and eat and eat without turning a tap to work any of it off. I've even lost my suntan.

Something keeps telling me my work is done for this term. I'm not sure if the Lord is preparing me or the devil is threatening me!

June 3rd

The Richardsons from a Mission eight hours north of us spent the night here on their way to Monrovia, then home for furlough. Nice people from North Carolina.

No news. I don't feel so bad—just not enough strength to do the work, and I've rested since February!

June 10th

I'm feeling stronger every day—someone has touched God for me, even though I have my "good" and "not so good" days. I was discouraged, but the "not so good" days are getting fewer and farther apart. I'm now able to oversee flower planting, cooking, and other "small thing." (Liberian for little things)

I had the best dream—thought I slipped in on you girls while you were cleaning house for my homecoming. I hugged and kissed you, so real! As much as I want to see you, I'd rather be able to finish my term, and not feel like a failure.

There's so much expense getting missionaries to the field, I'll be happy if I can stay. By faith, then, please send the denture cleaner any time—I'm out!

June 23rd

Still improving. I wanted to hear from God before I left my post of duty. I believe I know His will now, I will stay. I may not be able to make as many long treks as before, but there is plenty 'small thing' I can do.

I preached for the first time in a long time Sunday night and four received the Holy Ghost—makes seventeen this month.

July 6th

I went with Pauline and Reggie to Monrovia last week, took the plunge and had new teeth made. We went to Firestone for groceries—they had cabbage and carrots, first I've seen.

We were certainly on an outing. The passenger truck was not running between St. Paul River and Monrovia so we came back by Suehn. We spent Saturday night there and walked seven and a half hours Sunday (the fourth) to Maheh. Now I know how a ninety-year-old woman feels when she gets up and tries to straighten her humped back! I came on to Bomi Monday.

The seventh of July she felt far enough out of the shadows to write the first long letter to the Dugans, Grapel and other friends who faithfully supported their missionary without hearing from her personally for many months.

She told them about a trip to the Northeast border of Liberia they made with the Congos, missionaries with C. T. Studd's group.

There is a good clear road across Liberia in that direction, so there are many Mission stations. We spent the night at a Methodist Mission with a precious young couple only recently married. When I see so many young people without the Holy Ghost, eager to come and share the little they have, I cannot understand our Pentecostal young people standing back without making one move to reach those who have never heard the Full Gospel. They may never hear unless someone looks on the Harvest. Maybe our funds are limited, but, our God is not! If workers were willing to go—surely the Spirit would move on willing givers to send them.

FLASH! Our truck is here! A one ton green Chevrolet pick-up. We can't get it to the Mission until the barge on the St. Paul's river is repaired, but we are as excited as little children about it! We have had eighteen months of 'head-toting,' then catch as catch can' transport with 'head-toting' in between for several months. I feel this pick-up will open a whole new vista of progress for the work in Liberia. Thank God!

Chapter 12

MOVING ON!

Expansion seemed impossible when the school reached the government's limit of forty-five pupils for one teacher. They were turning students away, and the mine planned to hire two thousand more workers, meaning more families! The prayer request went out, "A second teacher needed!"

July 10th

Dear Friends,

The bounty of boxes we've received from all of you are a blessing—especially since our checks were very late last month. The malted milk and cake mixes were extra treats, and we could stand a repeat order of that small package of marshmallows. They were delicious toasted over the lamp at night. Wait a bit, in the light of the things I've been teaching on Paul's hardship's—I'm ashamed of asking—if I had more paper and time I'd start another letter ***without*** *that request!*

It was difficult for many of our older boys and girls to keep clean without a change of clothes, the boxes of clothing have met their need—they are grateful and so are we!

Two adults received the Holy Ghost speaking distinct English in a village recently—definitely other tongues for them.

Loose dentures hindered me preaching in the Spirit, but I've been unshackled by a brand new set of teeth. I've sneezed and they didn't fly out—the acid test will come when I get in a red-hot native service under a heavy anointing.

We rejoiced Sunday as twelve precious souls took the Name of Jesus in Baptism. Quite a few villagers are ready for baptism, too.

I'm regaining my strength. Thanks for your prayers, I really want to finish my term—only possible if you all continue to pray.

Great excitement swept the Mission when Mother Robinson drove the new pick-up from Monrovia to Bomi Hills, the third week of July. That was Halleulah Day! The green machine edged into its own mud house with sing-song hums of awe and a chorus of "Fine-Oh!"

Joseph, a young worker went to Bugbay that week and people surrounded him as he entered the village.

"Our Chief got the Holy Ghost and we want it, too!"

Three received the Spirit in an immediate prayer meeting before the service started.

Later, the chief and nine others were baptized in an early morning service in spite of village elders who spent the night inquiring of the dead and trying to deceive the people.

July the 26th, a holiday similar to the American fourth of July was celebrated with a high pitch of excitement, drums beaten and gourds rattled. While Gladys tried in vain to write letters, she remembered Vietown.

"How thankful I am we are not living in that hut as we did last year! In the U.S. firecrackers explode and its over with, but the tom toms beat on and on and the gourds rattle without stopping until late at night!"

She listened to Pauline's Bible Class in the living room singing 'Higher Ground' and thought, "What a contrast to the frenzy around us!"

August 13th, Bomi Hills
Dear Children,

This is a cool, rainy evening—I'm just like the natives now, if the temperature dropped to 70 degrees I'd freeze, for sure! The Mission is swarming with the relatives of the mission family. These are sociable people.

Pauline and I walked to Maheh Tuesday. I've had a stitch in my back since—moving around bent over for four days. Getting gradually better—and straighter.

The Ward's fall catalog has come and old and young enjoy a glimpse of the strange world they find in its pages.

Kenny's funiture - making talent has provided a large bookcase that divides dining-living areas, desk, coffee table, lamp table, victrola cabinet and "what not" shelf.

You asked for a Christmas list. You and the

folks at Nashville send so much I'm ashamed to mention my needs. I could use black leather dress pumps, or a purse, or hose, or cushion-sole house shoes. Our best Christmas gift would be some helpers—lack of workers holds us back. We don't know what will happen when Reggie goes home—probably one of us will take care of Maheh.

We couldn't get to Bugbay, water too high in the swamps between here and there.

Unusual visitors have spent a month at Bomi Hills—the Olsons, a young couple from Denmark collected animals and reptiles for a zoo.

Pauline is playing "Unclouded Day" on the victrola and I'm thinking about my children. I seldom hear from Allan and Verla.

Amazing News! Gladys' baby, Carmen, married Norman Harper. Part of the price a missionary pays for obeying God is being absent and far away on such tender occasions.

August 26th, Bomi Hills

Dear Family!

Rain has hardly let up all day. This was flag day, but the patriotic program planned by the teacher was rained out. We made frozen suckers for the children from Koolade with small bamboo sticks for handles. We'll save them and hope for tomorrow night. I'm teaching Bible in the school this semester and enjoying it, but Liberian English is so different, Paul or Viola have to 'break down' the lessons in order for everyone to understand.

Richard dreamed about receiving the Holy Ghost for two nights and it happened Sunday in the most unusual way. The Lord told him he would preach the Gospel. He has been helping on the Mission to pay his school tuition. We hope he'll make a worker in the future.

Pauline had a short bout with Malaria. Reverend Congo made the Mission his base for a three day hunting trip. The ladies enjoyed the tithe of his success!

September 10th, Bomi

Dear Little Girl,

Sometimes, letters come quickly. I am answering yours written September the first!

The young Lebanese man who was here with Reverend Congo came again and brought our mail yesterday. Fred came to Liberia two years ago from Lebanon as a merchant and professional gambler. His people are Catholic and Moslem. A few weeks ago someone took him to church where he repented, threw away his cigarettes and liquor, and quit gambling. He startled his fellow countrymen in Liberia by witnessing against these things. His family in Lebanon have disowned him, but, Reverend Congo befriended him and thinks he is genuine. After visiting here last week he felt led to work in this section. He bought $2,000.00 of goods to open a store for a native man to run for his support while he works for the Lord.

We thought he was open-hearted enough to accept the Holy Ghost so waited for a chance to tell him about it. The opportunity came when he asked us why there are so many different churches. After we explained the happenings on the Day of Pentecost, Pauline and I both told him how the Lord filled us with the Holy Ghost speaking in tongues. He was astonished and wondered why no one told him before. He declared, "Before I sleep tonight, I must receive the Holy Ghost."

While storing his supplies he stopped work and came over to us again. "How long does it stay on a person?" He asked uneasily. We finally understood he was talking about the Holy Ghost and explained everything to him according to the Word of God.

An old Canadian lady he met in Monrovia became ill on a visit to Reggie, so he decided to go see her at Maheh. He reminded us three or four times to pray for him at 8:00 p.m. for he believed that's when he would get the Holy Ghost. When we prayed here, several of our bunch was refilled or greatly blessed, but we won't hear from Fred until he returns tomorrow.

I'm rich again with packages from you, Sybil and Lucille. Everything needed and appreciated. There was a beautiful two piece blue silk dress in Sybil's box I wondered about, but Carmen's letter explained, she bought it for me and asked Sybil to send it. I really like it—a perfect fit.

Marie, the pictures were a flash, I'll try again before I come home.

Love to both of you, Mother

p.s. September 11th. Fred received the Holy Ghost at 8:00 p.m. last night and rejoiced the rest of the night!

September 19th, Bomi Hills
Dear Children,

I've just returned from teaching my class on the life of Christ. The children have Bible teaching six days a week. I hope we see the results someday.

Our weekend services were very good. Fred brought the young man who works for him from Monrovia—about eighteen years old. He received the Holy Ghost speaking Arabic, Fred's own language. Fred interpreted to us as the boy worshipped in a language foreign to him!

Fred's sister teaches philosophy in four different universities in the city where she lives. His family must be very wealthy, he mentioned recently the thousand dollar checks his mother used to send him for gambling. Just before he was saved, his parents wrote him to come home, he wouldn't have to work, their wealth was at his disposal. Now, he has chosen Christ and missionary work in the jungle so they have disinherited him. They asked that he never write them again, though his mother seems more lenient. He's only twenty-three years old. The Lebanese people here think he's crazy.

I went to Buleswa last week for our first service there in answer to a request from the Chief. The people are hungry—there was good response.

Reggie had boat reservations for November the 1st but decided to go by plane instead. Mother Holmes leaves today for the U.S.A.

I'm alright, all of us stay busy—yet cannot keep up with the work.

Children, this letter is full of love.

By the end of October, the breakthrough came at Buleswa when a young man of the Mendy Tribe received the Holy Ghost, the first of many to pray through. The villagers proudly showed Gladys the church they were building. It was actually a small, crude affair, but she was thrilled since they built on their own initiative without asking for help.

A stranger was present and asked to testify after the message.

"Many years ago," he said, "God spoke to me in a dream telling me how to live and that I must go back to my people and tell them to pray to God. I didn't go because I couldn't understand. Now, at last, God has sent someone to show us the way." Tears rolled down his face as he spoke. Gladys rejoiced to learn he was the son of the leper lady at Bolah who died two months after she was converted.

October 31st, Bomi Hills
Dear Children,

I received my Christmas box Saturday. I failed to resist the temptation to open the box of shoes. I told Pauline I didn't know if I could walk humbly or not if I put them on—my first dress show in two and a half years! The walking shoes Nilah is sending are not here yet, and I'm really needing them. These are so comfortable, fit perfectly with good steel arches, I'm tempted to take no thought for the morrow and wear them on the Mission, and around the house.

Comfort is getting to be a better helper every day, she'll be so proud of her fine red hat. We will have the canned oysters and cranberry sauce for Thanksgiving.

I received a letter from Esther Turnbow, their church at Bethel Springs sent a $40.00 offering. I've written them a long letter and took them on a trip with us to Buleswa. The Chief's daughter received the Holy Ghost yesterday.

Reggie is taking your package to mail for me. I've sent two native shopping bags. What you will think is a wooden fork is actually a native comb. I hope you enjoy the wild cherry jam—the only thing growing in the jungle suitable for jam. These grow in clusters on inch long stems up and down the tree trunk. I hope the package comes in time for your Christmas breakfast. I wanted to send some big bird feathers, but, not one bird came around!

We haven't heard of any help coming our way, and Oh, how we need helpers!

There were two big days back to back. St. Paul's River bridge was officially opened November the 15th. The President, all officials and everyone who owned a vehicle came to Bomi Hills that day. Many of them toured the Mission. School closed the next day with a 'cook' for all the children; dried fish soup, collard green soup, rice, jello and a biscuit (cookie) each. Reggie and a group of the children came for the closing program that night pronounced excellent by all who attended. Reggie brought Ruthie, nearly three years old, to rejoin her Christian parents who gave her to the Mission as a tiny baby when they were desperate and far from God.

The eventful days were crowned by a letter with the best possible news—the Pettys were appointed to return to Liberia!

December 13th, Bomi Hills
Dear Little Girl,

Pauline is moving to Maheh—how I'll miss her! We will take a truck load of things for Pauline to Gbelli Road and load up Reggie's luggage there to take her to Monrovia and Robert's Field to fly out to New York. Her children will meet her in Memphis—I can imagine the joy—can't you? Well, our time is coming, in God's will.

I've just jumped in debt again for $50.00 to Reggie for a bed, springs, mattress, net, a comfortable chair, the army cot I've borrowed ever since I've been here, and a tub big enough to sit down in and bathe. Something else to worry about until it's paid, but I need the things.

I wish all of my children could be together for Christmas. How I would love to see you!

The only excitement on the trip to see Reggie off happened as Gladys returned, not far from the Mission. She thought it was a huge leopard sitting in the middle of the road. When she came nearer saw it was a wildcat who seemed dazed by the bright lights. Then he leaped with graceful bounds into the bushes and was gone.

Gladys and helpers celebrated Christmas with a long table of refreshments on the back porch for the Gospel workers, the teacher and workmen and their families, and school boys and girls that lived on the Mission. Twenty-eight of them enjoyed 'American way' raisin pie, doughnuts and koolade together, before they gathered for the 'family' Christmas service and received the gifts provided by thoughtful people across the sea.

Pauline's hands were full with the palaver at Maheh—taking charge just before Christmas made it impossible for her to visit Gladys for Christmas dinner. Roast duck and dressing with cranberry sauce sounded good until Gladys sat down alone to eat her third Christmas dinner in Africa. Too exhausted to walk to Maheh she made the only gesture possible and sent Pauline half of the dinner. Both ladies were thankful when the Holidays were over!

One of the shadows over the festivities was the abduction of workman Robert by the Devil Bush Society. Strictly speaking he was not taken forcibly as much as intimidated until he feared not to go. His wife expected a baby and Gladys felt the defect keenly. The whole Mission joined in earnest prayer and fasting for his release.

1950

Gladys called the mine camp satan's stronghold, for response there was less than any other place. She tackled it with new determination and fervor on the first day of the New Year with charts and pictures illustrating a message on "The Lamb of God." She measured the service 'profitable.'

Robert was miraculously returned to the Mission the first week of January, just after his son was born. All their other babies died, Gladys made an extra effort to change his wife from the old country ways hoping they could pull this baby through. They named him Kenny Dare.

January 16th, Bomi Hills
Dear Children,

We have not sent nor received mail for two weeks. Pauline and I plan to go to Monrovia in the truck this week if we can get a pass from the company in time. I hope there's lots of mail waiting for us!

I yielded to temptation and took the black pumps for everyday wear. The leather soles were gone in three weeks, I've had rubber soles and heel caps put on so I can use them for walking. I think he used an old tire for there is a nice white fringe all around the edges but they are very comfortable.

I'm glad the carved elephants and skins arrived in time for your Christmas, though I'm sure they didn't look Christmassy!

John David is really cute now. He loves bread and the only place he gets it is at my house, when he hears my dinner bell he comes trotting—Ruthie joins him since she is here.

Rebecca helps me now, Viola went with

Pauline to Maheh. Comfort is quiet and sweet, she does the washing and cleaning.

You may have missed a couple of letters from me—you haven't commented on our building project. We completed the new school and started a church building hoping to finish by Easter. It is unsatisfactory having the school and church in the same building. I've alternated today between letter writing and hauling clay and water for daubing the church walls. It will not resemble the Nashville church, but it will be 'ritzy' mud church.

Nilah and Charlotte sent a Sunday night offering from their revival in Tulsa - $125.00. What a lift! Should finish it, except for the benches.

Marie, do you remember me mentioning Joel, a Maheh mission boy? He was a Vie, about nineteen years old. He wanted to come to Bomi, but I didn't think it fair to ask for him. He never came without bringing me flowers from the bush. A week ago he brought some so sweet smelling they perfumed the whole house. I never dreamed they would be the last. Joel died a few days ago of yellow jaundice. One cannot help but wonder, "Why the best?" The Lord has His reasons and someday we will understand.

Thanks again to my little girl and my son for the shoes, candy and magazines. I'll be writing the faithful at Nashville soon. I seldom get caught up with answering letters, but love to get them. Would love to see you—time is passing —just wait!

Long before the middle of February, school starting time, the problem of the last school year surfaced—too many students. Gladys didn't want to turn any of them away and wrote a specific appeal to Brother Stairs. Before there was time for a reply, the next mail brought a letter from a group of young people offering support for an extra teacher!

Toward the end of January she weighed the desire for a visit with Pauline against a stack of letters waiting for answers. Correspondence lost to a delightful day at Maheh, her second time there since Pauline assumed responsibility of the Mission.

February 9th, Bomi Hill
Dear Children,

Quite a stretch since you heard from me—just can't afford to send letters and mail every week.

William and Cooper are repairing the front of the house under the eaves. I opened the front door and there was William dangling in the door holding with all his might to the end of a rafter. He stood on a bamboo ladder propped against the door until I opened it and knocked the ladder out from under him. He was too astonished to yell and had to hang on 'till I replaced the ladder, laughing all the while.

We're still working on the church, I sadly underestimated the cost, but, Nilah and Charlotte sent another $125.00, Hallelujah!

The Mine Company required a pass for each trip

on the road they built to Monrovia, a time-consuming chore. When a new manager came, an American from Republic Steel in Cleveland, Ohio, Pauline and Gladys introduced themselves and asked if it would be possible to get a pass good for a year. They left the office rejoicing when their request was granted. Trips to bring supplies and mail could be made whenever money for gasoline was available. Though sending a messenger by truck or driving cost the same, they would continue sending one every second or third week to save their strength, it was comforting to know they were free to go anytime in case of need.

March 5th
Dear Children,

I wonder if my family got together today as planned? I hope so!

Heavy rain has washed the dust away, cooled the air and started the grass to green.

Two leopards came in the house yesterday! Sounds scary-thrilling until I explain, they were carried in, cubs and ever so cute.

I took a new girl today, formerly from Dr. Jones' Mission. Her name is Ella, and she will share a room in the house with Rebecca and Comfort. Comfort and her red hat is so amusing. She keeps it wrapped in tissue, carefully hid away in the dressing table Kenny made for me. They usually keep their things in the place I allot them, but that hat is special!

I took Rebecca to Monrovia—she has now seen the world and the waters thereof! When we went upstairs to the State Treasury Department,

I had to help her ***back*** *down the stairs. Everyone who saw us thought she was about to faint.*

Rea, I appreciate the $5.00 a month you've been giving on the bill I owe Reggie.

I suppose you are in your new home, things move fast in America. It took me five months to get a mud shanty built. We are still working on a better church building and don't know when it will be finished.

Carpenters started making the doors and windows for the new building by the middle of March, but enervating heat restrained the pace of everything on the Mission to snail-slow.

March 22nd, Bomi Hills
Dear Children,

We have a cool, breezy, cloudy day—the most pleasant for a long time. I can't complain about the weather, except I'm afraid the rains will come before we are ready. Three buildings are not properly thatched, have to be reworked making the thatch thicker. Birmah, Robert and Mono go to the swamp daily for thatch and the school boys go after school to help carry it in.

They have cut the "bush" in front of the Mission—almost makes us feel like we have moved. We still have our own bush on one side and back of us. We seldom see monkeys playing in the tree tops now, they have killed so many for chop.

There haven't been many boxes lately, but one came from Evansville that had four dresses in it that I can wear. I was needing some, nothing lasts long here.

From a letter April 4th

I've had another round of malaria, small-small—just felt uncomfortable for a few days.

I'm so far behind with work and letter writing, I'll be ashamed to face people at home. It's just as well nothing more has been mentioned about my furlough. Yes, Nashville is my home church but I hope they forget about a homecoming service. The Lord and I both know I haven't done anything outstanding to deserve such honor.

I'm glad to hear I'll have a machine to sew on when I come home, although what I had in mind was a big, soft easy chair with a hassock to prop my feet on!

April 15th, Bomi Hills
Dear Children,

Just returned from Bugbay noon today. We had two services there, one at Bolah and one at Sister Marshall's village. The sun was so hot, we thought we would melt, but we didn't. Now, I'm sitting at my desk sipping iced pineapple juice like a civilized lady of leisure!

What a turnout for our Easter program last Sunday night! The Secretary of the Interior was in Council meetings in Klay so he came with three District Commissioners, four Paramount Chiefs, many Clan Chiefs, and other officials.

We had a crowd for true! And the new church was not ready. The Secretary said it was unbelievable so much had been accomplished in less than two years. He pronounced the arrangement of the buildings on the Mission ground "very picturesque!" He represented Liberia at the United Nation's Council in New York last September. The Big Chiefs said "their hearts were satisfied," which means complete approval.

They gave us a special invitation to attend their business meeting in Klay. Pauline and I drove down Monday afternoon to show ourselves friendly. We ate lunch with the Secretary and everyone treated us royally. I took some ice to the District Commissioner's wife where they are staying.

They will visit Maheh Saturday morning. Pauline will serve refreshments and I'm sure she is stewing. I would have been with a warning about their coming, but they came to us unexpectedly. To my surprise, I felt at ease with them.

Vinnah just came in, plunked John David on the floor so she could pick the jiggers out of his feet. He throws a fit at her house, but if I'm near, he never whimpers.

Your package came. The dress is so pretty and just fits. I'm saving it and the gloves for my homecoming. I had a notion to dress up and sit before the mirror a while but decided that wasn't practical, I'd soon have to come back to earth.

I received the Herald with pictures of Reggie's homecoming service. I'm a little uneasy about this homecoming fanfare. I'll feel "at home" and "welcome" without being put up higher than I belong. I would prefer a regular service with one of Brother Wallace's good messages and the privilege of sitting in my old place. How I would enjoy a good Nashville service right now!

On her first visit to a new village Gladys was challenged by the Chief.

"My ju ju (witchpower) is stronger than yours," he said, "See this man laying face upward on the ground? I have power to lift him by my word and hold him in the air as stiff as a log. If your Jesus is so powerful, let him help you push the man back to the ground!"

Sure enough, on the Chief's word the man was raised about two feet off the ground. She placed both hands on him and pushed down, "In the Name of Jesus!" she commanded. He settled to the ground. The Chief ordered, "Raise!" and he floated in mid air. The Name of Jesus brought him down again! When the Chief's command suspended him in the air the third time, she cried, "Lord Jesus, in your great Name, bring him to the ground and break the evil power that holds him!" She knelt by him as he fell at her feet. He was delivered from Satan's might, began to worship Jesus and in a few minutes began to speak in other tongues as the Spirit gave the utterance, the first fruit of the harvest of souls in that village.

Box 44, Monrovia

April 19th

You never fail me Marie, and this week I received three fat letters from Carmen. I'm thankful she and Norman are happy. The news of Allan and Verla's divorce shocked me, though all I can do is pray.

We've been gardening this week. We have a rich spot to which I committed a lot of American seed we got from the Agricultural Department.

From the whispered talk going on around here you can rest assured my birthday next month will be properly celebrated. I overheard Comfort suggest they "get mother away for that day." I presume the doings is to be a surprise, or else they want to be sure I don't put my mouth or hand there to restrain them.

The Council meeting at Klay ended last Saturday. The secretary and several 'big shots' are coming to the mine office in cars and trucks, then they plan to make a six hour hammock journey to Gbarmah. That will be a nice trip in this rain over those swamps. When he leaves the highway and goes through the bush for six hours, he'll know he's been somewhere. I've been wishing he would find occasion to travel that path, we go over part of it to Bugbay and Bolah. I thought maybe some of the tree trunks might be moved, in that case, and the "rolling bridges" made a bit more stationery.

p.s. Could you find an old hat for Rebecca?

Pauline always went with Gladys on the trips to Monrovia, often spent the night with her to keep from walking to the highway before daylight. Her heavy work load hindered socializing, but Gladys spent the 6th of May at Maheh, only the third visit since Reggie left. She was concerned about Pauline who was working hard with building and repair projects besides the other usual work of the Mission.

May 17th

Well, children, this is the day. Things are humming in the kitchen. Judging from sounds and smells, we are going to have sweet bread (cake) with fresh coconut icing, and rice with fish soup. The last named is better than it sounds deliciously flavored with palm oil. The girls presented me with a beautiful bouquet at breakfast this morning with a sweet note. They will eat with me today but I think they're baking enough cake for everyone on the Mission. It is now 2:00 p.m. and I'm starving, Comfort is setting the table, maybe it won't be long.

5:00 p.m. Well, the girls really did it up brown! While I was writing Comfort came to fix my hair before dinner. My head is a bit sore from the change, but it was part of the plans, so I couldn't change them, even to save my head. She did my hair with half in a knot on my neck, the other half pulled up in high affair with two red celluloid bows and smaller bows of pink and green yarn. Everyone on the Mission has concluded Comfort has a talent for doing hair! The girls put on their best clothes and invited Lajetta to eat with us.

A blowing rain came up and we had to close the shutters at the close of the meal, making it dark in the house. They lit candles and sang "Happy Birthday." Bless their hearts they did their best and I appreciated it. They made some little gifts for me that represented a lot of love. I still missed my children.

Gladys did not look for Mount Carmel contests however, when they came she knew she must stand her ground in the Name of Jesus.

"You say your Jesus has all power," the witch-doctor - Chief sneered, "Can you handle this deadly snake? My ju ju protects me from his bite—if your God cannot take care of you, we do not want to listen to his Book!"

She shivered with cold prickles of fear watching the revolting, twisting loops and darting tongue of the ugliest snake she had ever seen twining around the Chief's neck and arms. She remembered promises, "Lo, I am with you, always, . . . " "they shall take up serpents; and if they drink any deadly thing, it shall not hurt them . . . . "

Over and over God had proven His grace sufficient but that thought did not check the violent pounding of her heart. She wondered which would be worse, to die of a heart attack or from snake bite, neither would glorify God. There was really no choice. A whole tribe was at stake—if they were ever to hear the living Gospel the challenge must be met. Breathing the Name of Jesus she stepped forward and reached for the snake. When she touched it the power of God swept away fear. The Chief's eyes widened in

Old Pastor

astonishment—as the snake lay quiet and calm in her hands.

With that victory another wide door swung open. The ex-witchdoctor Chief soon became the Spirit filled leader of his village where many were born again.

May 24th

Dear Children,

I feel like I've been on a merry-go-round this week. The mat makers for the church are here, the workmen are building an outdoor kitchen for Birmah and Vinnah and the boys are plastering the church with cream colored mud. I try to make the rounds regularly. If I don't keep an eye on them, I know I'll wish I had.

The mats are painted and up in the gable end of the church—I'll take a picture when I get some film. We bush people think it's a swell church, but don't expect too much from the American point of view. It's only mud, sticks and mats.

A message just came to meet Pauline at Gbelli road 5:00 p.m. She will sleep here so we can leave early for Monrovia. I'm glad for her to come and share my luxuries—leaf lettuce and radishes, there should have been mustard greens but the bugs stripped the stalks.

Yesterday I looked up and saw a strange woman staggering up my path. It was a missionary from six days in the interior, she had walked most of the way. The carriers who started with her ran away, she walked on alone.

Her feet are so sore today she can hardly move. She is by herself on her station, no other missionary near and hasn't received mail for six months. We will take her to Monrovia tomorrow, her name is Canady.

I haven't heard from the Board. Someone said Gene Bailey from Tulsa is applying to come to Liberia. We can use her, we also need a couple—a man to oversee the work would be a blessing from God. When the Lord gets ready for me to come home, He'll make it possible. His way and time is best.

Chapter 13
WHO AND WHEN?

June 1st

Children,

I'm speechless! The news of Carmen's baby daughter reached me May 29th. I've thought several times I should tell you the quickest way to get a message to me would be through Liberian Mining Company, Bomi Hills by cable.

I don't know what I would have done had I known—like I've learned to do about everything else, I guess—leave it in the hands of the Lord and trust Him to work it out.

Now, I want to know all about it. There's so many questions. Is Carmen all right? Does the baby look like her, and what is her name? Your letter written when she was only three hours old didn't give Grandma enough details!

Brother Stairs wrote asking what I thought about a furlough—said the Board did not want anyone to stay over three years in the tropics if they can help it. But, they don't know what to do about someone to take my place. I've answered that I feel both the Mission and I will need a change when my time is up in August. The Mission needs someone with new fire and energy to push things forward and I could surely enjoy a rest in one of those platform rockers.

I'll be eager to hear that all is well.

Word came about June the 8th that all was well. Marie said, "The baby's name is Suzanne and she looks just like her mother!"

Building and building repair inched on. The Mission house received another coat of clay plaster, cream color this time. The woodwork was repainted blue. Every house on the Mission was trimmed with a different color, brightening their jungle acreage.

June 17th

Dear Children,

I received a letter from Carmen written June 7th. Now, I look forward to seeing another little granddaughter!

I can hardly believe I haven't written since the package came. The shoes are not only pretty, but fit perfectly. Rebecca brightened the church Sunday morning in the flowered hat you sent. We have a budding romance on the Mission. She and Paul want to get engaged. They will make an ideal couple—he is a fine young man and has walked straight.

I don't think I told you about the snake battle at Maheh Mission. Nobody hurt, just scared, as you may know when I tell you they got out the 30-30, the 22 and the 12 gauge shotgun. And the snakes got safely away after two hours of war!

Pauline came over for the first time on Sunday last week, we planned to leave early Monday for Monrovia. About 5:00 p.m. a "strong breeze" (as the natives called it) hit us. The "strongest breeze" I've ever been in. The school house and the building we used for services were flattened to the ground, even the seats smashed. The new church roof made of palm leaf cords was damaged and leaking all over, and it's not even finished! In the midst of the confusion someone yelled that the teacher's house was blown down and Lajetta was standing out in the storm dazed. No one was hurt but we had to move her possessions to the Mission house in the rain. The metal roof probably saved this house, if it were roofed with cords, everything could have been ruined by the storm. All the other roofs were damaged, a tree fell across the toilet and the chicken house roofs. Such "breezes" are rare in Liberia, most of those on the Mission had never seen anything like this before.

I put all the boys to work Monday, Tuesday and Wednesday repairing damages and school continued in the new church from Wednesday. We have an enrollment of sixty now.

I haven't heard from Brother Stairs since I wrote him that I felt both the mission and me needed a change. I don't have energy to go to the villages as often as I would like. I'm not sick, but my blood pressure is low and anyone in the tropics this long has enough malaria in their system to have a "dragged-out" feeling. I can't be as zealous as I want to be, but I believe, until help comes, the Lord will give me strength to keep the ball rolling—gently—at least.

p.s. Have you heard from Allan? He wrote me he's getting married June 24th to a girl named Rosetta. I'm still sorry he and Verla couldn't make it.

June 25th

I've felt for several weeks the deteriorating surroundings of our temporary building dampened worship. The "breeze" eliminated the makeshift and put us in the new church. Though the interior isn't finished, all of us agree the services are more blest.

The new records from Indianapolis are so good—I especially enjoy Jean and Nathan Urshan's singing.

Pauline has been sick with strep throat this week. I bruised the bottom of my foot and couldn't walk from the road to go see her. She's better, I'll meet her at Gbelli road this afternoon so we can leave early in the morning for Monrovia.

I've no idea WHO will take my place or WHEN my furlough will be, but I'm resting easy.

Paul and the other boys have come in to listen to the new records and my writing inspiration has vanished. I'll write Carmen a note, put everyone else off for another week, as usual, and rest awhile.

July 2nd

Dear Marie,

Two mail trips have passed, and no letter from you. I hope vacation is over and you can catch up with your foreign correspondence again!

I received a letter the Board is trying to find a replacement for me.

Pauline, her teacher and all the girls are here to spend the night. She will preach for us and it's almost church time.

Pauline knew well the heavy toll of the tropics on North Americans and realized her colleague needed the furlough that was due. She offered to try supervise both Missions while Gladys went home—having the truck, and the road to Maheh nearly completed would make it possible. Gladys knew that would be an inhuman load but communicated the offer to the Board as Pauline requested.

July 20th

Dearest children,

I haven't heard much from you lately, but we're going down tomorrow hoping . . .! The thought of letters spurs us on.

I have some grass mats boxed, ready to send. I'd love to get some small souvenirs for the Missionary band, but don't know if I can. Don't expect much from me and Liberia, Darlings.

Paul and Rebecca are engaged and happy as larks. We want to give them a mission wedding and hope it happens before I leave. He is a good carpenter and wants to make their furniture.

Box 44, Monrovia

I spent a day at Maheh this week. Seeing Pauline every week or so on our trips to town, I've spared myself the walking, but was afraid she would feel bad so went. Just as I came back, Sister Teasley, a colored missionary and nine grown boys and girls came by to spend the night with us on their way to a Mission eight hours north of us. They will stay with us on their return tonight. I expect Sister Martin tomorrow.

I've heard from many of the faithful folks at Nashville. If anything has been accomplished here, it's because of the good help and encouragement I've received.

From a letter to Marie, July 27th

Four days until your birthday, and three years since I saw you! I don't think it will be long before I see you again, though there's no word about my furlough.

Your letter with the sage in it didn't come, but never mind, Firestone finally got some in. Besides, every duck on the place turned up their toes and died within a few hours, except two babies and a mother duck who is setting. I had the drake for dinner before all this happened, but it'll be awhile before I eat duck again.

These young people start humming when they are excited or frightened. A loud concert of "Uh-m-m-m-m-'s" yesterday morning sent me out to investigate. The boys were cutting grass and discovered a huge snake in a tree near the house. They chunked that thing for thirty minutes or longer trying to get him down. They were scared enough, I figured they would all take off with their hoes, poles and cutlasses, if he came down suddenly. But, the snake was so mad he coiled 'round and 'round in the top of the tree with his tongue darting out until the boys worked up such a frenzy, they were ready for him when he slid to the ground. Thomas, who is usually quiet, struck at him with a fifteen foot pole, missing each lick and yelling, "I got him, I got him!" Four or five of them finally did get him. He was over six feet long, light gray with almost white spots and a wide flat head—a wicked looking thing!

Your package came last week, I was so glad for everything. I divided with Pauline, she doesn't have a sweet daughter sending her packages. She shares her boxes with me, too.

p.s. I've just been informed Mother Duck has hatched out five little ones.

The long-standing question of 'WHO' was answered early in August. Brother Petty's health had improved and the Petty family would be her replacement! 'WHEN' was still rather vague—they hoped to sail from New Orleans sometime after the October Conference. Still, the news replaced uncertainty with vitalizing hope.

The church was barely completed when the workmen started gathering poles for a new school on that bare end of the compound where the old school stood before it was blown down.

Paul and Rebecca's wedding was set for September the 30th. Previous plans for a Mission wedding ended in disappointment. Now both Mission families were excited about the prospect. Every package from America was checked for items suitable for outfitting the wedding party, first to materialize was a good blue suit for the groom.

From a letter to Carmen, September 2nd

Comfort and I staged a clean-up campaign today. Just have time for a short note before I prepare for tonight's Bible study.

The wedding is at 2:00 p.m. the 30th. Would you believe someone sent a wedding veil in a box? Another package yielded a pretty pair of white shoes Rebecca's size. But, when she gets excited she cannot say a word, I don't know how she will ever manage to say "I do" before a crowd!

A lady from Canada wrote she is interested in Africa. I wish I could have someone to work with me when I come back. It's much easier when two share the load. I hope Petty's will stay here even when I return. Bomi Hills needs him.

I'm getting so anxious to see all of you.

Several boxes came that supplied everything still needed for the wedding including a long embossed organdy white dress for the bride. All these treasures were laid out in the living room waiting for the big day. Gladys was in her room for a short rest when she heard giggles and peals of laughter from the back porch. She looked out. The prospective groom Paul had never worn shoes and decided he should try them. He walked up and down stepping high as if he were in deep water and didn't want to get his pants wet.

Gladys joined the unrepressed laughter and suggested a lot more practice was needed before time to walk down the aisle!

September 9th

Dear Rea and Glen

I know you are expecting news of my homecoming, but I haven't heard. The important thing is I want to see everyone of you the minute I hit the ground whenever it is. My glasses will look nice for the trip—held together with scotch tape over the nose and the right side drooping on my cheek, but they still serve their purpose.

I am being obedient and "taking it easy" according to instructions. I don't go to the villages anymore, but send the workers—though everything in me longs to go, as before.

We had a scare while we were in Monrovia, Monday. Construction on the new road has been held up by traffic, so all travel passes were cancelled. The company wanted to issue only a few passes. The Attorney General said,

"If one has a pass, all must have one." The manager at Brewersville said they could not possibly give us another pass.

We started home, but I told Pauline, we couldn't accept that. God gave us the truck to be ***used*** *not parked, so we went back to Monrovia to see the Attorney General personally. He was out of town for the day—we spent the night and* *got an appointment with him the next day. Thank God, we won our case because of our Missions and schools—otherwise we would have been grounded until next April, and Pauline and Gladys would be walking again.*

How do you like the picture I sent of our fine mud church. I do wish we could afford aluminum roofing for it. The new teacher and his wife and baby live in the cottage beyond the church.

The man in the picture holding the poisonous snake (it's over eight feet long) is a member of the snake Society. They wear certain leaves and though the snake coils around them with its tongue flashing, it will not bite them. It isn't of the constrictor family, I've never heard of a leaf holding a constrictor in tow!

Kenny and Rachel from Maheh will be attendants at the wedding. Someone sent a light blue taffeta evening gown in a box of used clothes to Pauline that Rachel can wear for the occasion.

A two motor plane has just circled the mission twice very low. John David kicked and screamed. He never saw a flying car before! He thought trouble was over his head for true!

Robert has just brought in two pretty shells for you girls, large enough for wall vases.

I'll keep you posted.

The wedding was a grand affair, the teacher's nieces were flower girls and a goldsmith made the wedding ring from raw gold. The church was lavishly decorated with palm branches and flowers, and

Bienu

aside from the stars of the show being extremely nervous everything went smoothly. Paul had practiced enough to walk without stepping high!

October14th

Dear Children

We didn't receive one slip of mail last week—Pauline and I were put out of our serenity for true!

No, my little girl, you don't lay down that pen until I say so. Brother Stairs wrote from Jamaica that they didn't have fares for the Pettys to come or me to return. Three new missionaries have just gone out to other fields. Fares are not easily raised for those going out, much less coming home. Wouldn't it be something if I don't get home before Christmas?

The Pettys wrote they were hoping I'll still be here when they come so we can talk things over. That would be good. I'm eager to know when they are leaving, but didn't have passage the last I heard.

No doubt about it, the Lord's hand is in the delay, and my staying longer than the usual three years, so we will not fret.

School closes November the 15th with a program. It would be nice if the Pettys could be here by then. We are encouraging the believers from all the surrounding villages to gather in for a warm welcome service when they arrive.

The next trip to Monrovia witnessed a terrible sight. Two ladies from Suehn Mission lived in the

Congo's Mission while they were on furlough in Canada. Pauline and Gladys stayed there often when the Congo's were on station, and always enjoyed browsing through the Christian Bookstore on the ground floor.

Fire broke out on the second floor and the whole building, with a three story house jammed against it were quickly destroyed. Monrovia's only fire truck was in the garage for repairs, so they watched one big house after another disintegrate in hot flames. Finally, a ramshackle building second to the end of the block was pulled down and the fire brought under control leaving only one house standing on the block. Ironically, the town is almost completely surrounded by water with no means of using it to put out a fire. All business was suspended for three hours.

November 2nd

Dear Children,

A letter from the Pettys said they are packed and ready, waiting for passage. They're making Tupelo their headquarters until they get a sailing date. The earliest promise is December 14th, you know what that means don't you? But, it still won't be long. It will be so wonderful being together, we won't need any holidays to add to that.

This has been a big day, so many people there has no chance to write. Things have quietened down, now, I'm too tired.

November 5th

The mission is full of visitors, all going to

Monrovia with me tomorrow; Pauline and three boys from Maheh and Sister Canady and five boys and girls from six days in the interior. Sister Canady had a hard trip, came in crying when she arrived a little while ago. She has been on the road for a week because she didn't have the strength to keep moving. She slept two nights out in the huge Gola Forest unable to make it to a village. The villages are twelve hours apart through there. She is worrying now about me going home and losing her stopping over place, bless her heart!

Three received the Holy Ghost Friday night praise the Lord!

This is just a few lines Darlings to let you know everything is o.k.

November the fifteenth came and went without the Pettys, though the school closing was an impressive achievement.

Gladys welcomed a steady stream of travellers needing hospitality, remembering the many weary miles she had trudged through the jungle. She brought supplies to Bomi for Sister Hargrove from a mission eight hours north. Sister Martin from Grajeh Mission, Sister Canady from Congbi, Sister Jiles and others used the oasis she provided gratefully.

November 22nd

My Children,

It seemed so cool, I thought it must be down to 50 degrees, but the Mine office says the lowest recorded temperature is 68 degrees and that doesn't happen often. I guess I'll freeze when I get home, I've been wearing a head scarf and a sweater.

This is market day and pay day at the Mines. The natives for miles around bring their "small thing" to sell; egg plant, bitter balls, greens, etc. the people from the villages consider it their duty to come by the mission to pay their respects. They will be in and out all day. Some from Kowadee have just left.

The big news is the Pettys should arrive between the 10th and 15th of January. The Assembly of God plane is due the last day of that month. It usually stays three or four days and returns via South America. I hope I can go on it. If this works out, I'll need you all to meet me in Springfield, Missouri. Will that be possible?

I didn't expect to face the Christmas Palaver again this year, and I don't know of any Christmas boxes coming. Oh me! And anyone who has ever dashed me a butter pear or an okra pod (or anything else) expects a Christmas dash. All these school children just know Christmas will be something grand. The natives cannot be convinced that all white people are not rich beyond words. It's too late to ask for things to be sent. I must trust the Lord to help me, maybe He has already moved on someone to send what is needed!

Don't you send anything more than is already on the way. I'll keep you posted.

Gladys received a letter stating there was hopes

her fare would be in by the first of February so a tentative booking was made on the A. G. plane schedule to leave Roberts Field that day going to Springfield with one stop in South America.

When she noticed Thanksgiving Day on her calendar, she decided there should be a holiday. The whole mission family celebrated by walking to Maheh for a day with Pauline and the mission family there.

December 13th

We are enjoying a shower—so refreshing. The grass was brown and flowers were wilting. We are catching rainwater to use for daubing which will save me hauling it from the creek with the truck. We have to rework the boys' kitchen and the school is nearly ready to daub. We're getting the window frames this week.

You'll get this letter about Christmas—I trust yours will be blest. I'm wondering if I'm going to get through it and save face. I received a box of toys from a group of children in East Moline that will help a lot. I've decided to postpone Christmas to Monday so it will not extend over the whole weekend. Christmas away from you this time will not be so bad when I think that in little over a month we will be reunited. Let's celebrate then!

Time will fly. We're trying to get a lot done before the Pettys arrive. Even then, he will have plenty to do before the rainy season sets in—finishing the school, building their house etc., besides the Gospel work.

I'm not sending Christmas cards and letters will be spasmodic notes from here on. I hope my family will all be together for Christmas and have a nice one.

A cable said the Pettys would arrive January, the eighth. The same mail brought word the A. G. flights were cancelled indefinitely, sliding Gladys back to uncertainty on "when." She continued the waiting game with good grace.

December 21st

Dear Children,

Pettys have been on their way for a week—so much to do before they arrive. The throes of Christmas are not over, but soon will be. I think I may survive after all with the good Lord's help. There were several packages on my last trip to town that will save the day.

We had to stop work on the schoolhouse to get the other buildings in order. We thought the boys kitchen could be reworked, but it had to be rebuilt. The toilets and bathhouses must be rethatched. We have started a wash-iron kitchen. We are trying to get all of the building plastered inside and out. The clay has to be dug from pits in the swamp and that takes time.

Your lovely Christmas gifts came today, thanks so much.

January 7th, 1951

It is the day before the Pettys arrival. We have swept and garnished the house and Mission, built, roofed and reroofed for weeks trying to have everything in order. But, as quickly as possible the boys' house and the garage must have a new roof.

I haven't told you about Christmas yet. Well, we pulled through! Everyone seemed to feel it was appropriate and good. Imagine my surprise when Pauline sent me over the Parker pen I am writing this letter with. I don't know how she managed. I responded with a grand gesture and gave her a pair of my nylon stockings. She was needing some—I hope I can get home on the other pair.

If there's any news from the Board when I get to Monrovia in the morning I'll add it to this letter before I mail it.

Lots and love and kisses

p.s. Pettys are here—great folks. I'm relieved and glad.

Record crowds came out to welcome Brother and Sister Otis Petty and their daughter Lois Ann, back to Liberia. Gladys and the Pettys opened their hearts to each other in precious hours of fellowship and planning for the future of the work. Years later he wrote of his impressions on arrival.

We found Bomi Hills Mission carefully laid out with well-placed mud structure buildings and paths edged with rocks and flowering shrubs. It was evident much forethought and planning went into this by someone who really cared. Only determination and dedication could have won the tedious legal procedure to begin the Mission from Government offices, Native Commissioners, Chiefs and sub-Chiefs.

Gladys drove the pick-up into the jungle to haul thatch, poles and rattan for building. We saw her stand in the rain to oversee the work being done. The climate was warm and humid with or without rain. She often came in from a long hard day drenched with perspiration and sat down to a meal of rice and cassava greens. Then, after cleaning up, conducted a Gospel service on the Mission.

Her greatest delight was treks through the jungle with Gospel workers taking the Word of God to the outlying villages.

The Africans loved Mother Robinson very much, I'm sure it was because she loved them dearly and they felt it.

January 15th, no word.

January 18th, the ticket money came, along with tentative boat reservations.

Janury 20th

Darlings,

Here I am, all set, waiting for my ship to come in! Even have my suitcase packed and my hair washed. I'm booked on the "African Sun," Farwell lines, due in today, but delayed. Since I don't want an expensive wait in Monrovia, I'm staying here and keeping in contact with the agent.

I have completed the necessary formalities

and am ready to buy my ticket as soon as the boat is in the harbor. I won't mail this until I know the sailing date and we are about ready to leave. When you receive this, I'll probably be somewhere on the Atlantic, a few thousand miles nearer to you.

It will take eleven or twelve days to reach the U.S. and I may not know which port until two or three days before landing somewhere on the Eastern Coast. Cargo boats are not always predictable. I'll try to phone you after we land as to when and how I'll be coming in from the coast.

I don't know whether to look forward to the trip or dread it. Pettys were so seasick they dread it for me. Some of my missionary friends say, "Oh, it was wonderful!" Anyway, I can endure a lot knowing I'm on my way to see my children!

January 22nd Morning

Ship is in—expect to depart tomorrow. It doesn't stop any place on the way to the U.S. but it's possible there could be a delay in leaving. You may be hearing from me the 2nd or 3rd of February.

January 22nd Afternoon

Boarding now, to sail tomorrow morning.

January 24th

I've been on board two days. Making hurried trip to town to post this letting you know the ship has been delayed loading cargo. They expect to leave later today. I wanted you to know so you wouldn't worry.

Our port of arrival is New York, I've written Rubins to meet me—I'll call you from there.

They tell me we could be twelve or fourteen days crossing the Atlantic if the winds are contrary.

Longing to see you all!

Love and kisses,

Mother

Chapter 14
SWEPT UP!

The African Sun crossed the Atlantic on a fairly even keel except for a few minor squalls. A bone-weary missionary caught up on sleep and marked off slowly passing days. The last three approaching New York dragged interminably, but finally she steped off on home ground met by friends, the Rubins.

That long-awaited chance to phone her family was too exciting to be coherent. All that was understood was her arrival time at Nashville. She found it hard to believe she was actually there when the plane landed. Even hugging and being hugged, and baby-kisses of a cute little granddaughter seemed as one of those lovely dreams. She kept thinking, "I'll wake up in a minute back at Bomi!"

There was so much to catch up on—letters could never tell it all. Gladys confessed how difficult writing letters had been for her the last year and they rejoiced together to be free from the Box 44 routine for awhile.

She had a small taste of the dream about a big easy chair with a hassock to prop her feet on before the swirling vortex of deputation swept her away.

"Would you speak for us Wednesday night?"

"Come preach at our church Sunday!"

"There's this rally or Fellowship Meeting, that Mission Conference, campmeeting or convention . . . .!"

"Could you visit our school?"

Invitations came thick and fast. How could she say "no"? These were the people who loved and supported her, the ones she depended on for prayers that would keep the work moving. She wanted time to rest and think and prepare herself for the change of pace, but that was not to be. Rested and ready or not, there was no choice.

She began to understand—the missionary on furlough no longer belongs to one's family, or even to one's self. The missionary belongs to Mission Work and the life-and-death seriousness of the work requires everything; time, strength, inspiration and life itself on both sides of the world. She soon realized this was the only way to return to her field of labor and to gather the supplies she hoped to take with her.

Carmen once said, "Mother was always a 'pro' doing anything."

She tackled the deputation trail with reluctance keeping the fierce longing to be with her family as a permanent heart - fixture, gratified only on precious, but brief visits between services. Her genuine sincerity and anointed ministry brought her through as a "pro" but glimpses behind the scenes reveal some of the price she paid.

Although Gladys was an extrovert with an outgoing personality, facing strangers accentuated an acute inner loneliness. It didn't last long, but a thin veil of dread had to be snapped through in every new situation. One of the most jealously guarded secrets was her physical disability. Louise Dugan travelled with her part of the time on deputation. When weakness forced her to stop and rest while climbing a few steps, she insisted, "Louise don't tell Marie or anyone else, otherwise I might not get to go back—and I must return. You see, my heart is over there!"

Means of travel was uncertain and speaking frequently wearisome, however the greatest load she carried was the compelling burden to return. It was hard to understand her own feelings. While in Liberia she longed to come home, especially the last year there, and was barely here before this intense longing to return to the field siezed her, and never slackened its hold. Every true missionary becomes well acquainted with this paradox.

Gladys was grateful for the time that Norman and Carmen or Glenn and Marie could take her to services. It was a pleasure to be with old friends and a special joy to purchase equipment and supplies for Liberia. Up and down the country and around and around she went. Lasting impressions reached far beyond those missionary services. More than one missionary on the field has testified, "She was the first missionary I ever heard, and her life encouraged me to obey my call."

There was no doubt about the many unusual and

frightening experiences Gladys had on the field, but she refused the role of heroine. She told about times of danger beginning, "this happened to a lady I know . . . ." only admitting later under pressure from close friends that she was the lady.

Caught up in the whirl it seemed deputation had gone on for ages and would last forever, but nearing the end another prayer was answered. Gene Bailey from Tulsa was appointed to Liberia. She would not return alone, God provided a helper!

Many things were improved. Pan Am now had a regular schedule through West Africa eliminating the uncertain layover at Dakar. Gene benefited from Gladys on what should be done, and the supplies she would need. The responsibility of the Great Commission gripped more churches so finances for fares and equipment came a little easier.

The tedium of packing was done. Painful farewells eased by the peace of obedience were behind them. Gladys and Gene boarded Pan Am in New York for Roberts Field, Liberia the middle of March 1952.

Chapter 15
CIRCUMSTANCES AND GLORY!

1952

Humid tropical heat slapped them the minute the ladies walked down the steps of the plane at Roberts Field, but, nothing could faze the deep satisfaction that sang in the heart of Gladys, "I'm back, thank God! Oh, thank God!"

Immigration formalities and the usual red tape detained them two days in Monrovia. Brother Petty came March the 18th and brought them home to Bomi Hills Mission. They were not able to unpack their suitcases for four days. A steady stream of people came to welcome Gladys and the new missionary. Some laughed, others cried and many wailed an emotional response to her return.

Gladys wrote:

The heat really hurts, but I'll get used to it again in a few days. Such a drastic change from the weather when we left. I'm writing with one hand and wiping sweat with the other one. Gene says she is melting.

It looks like I'll be too busy to even think for a few days, there is much work to do. One hundred and eight pupils in school.

They are getting telephone service in Monrovia on a small scale—maybe in two or three years we can call.

By April she was settled in familiar routine. Large crowds packed the Mission church for every service. New teaching aids were received with enthusiasm and fruitful response. Gladys offered to free Brother Petty for more important tasks by taking over supervision of the continual building and repair. The teachers needed better accomodation; by faith, she started a two-apartment building for them.

Since Georgia returned from furlough Pauline made Bomi Hills her base, it was closer to the evangelistic outreach on her heart. Fassama Mission was her dream that later came true.

Gladys was anxious to begin village treks again and decided to start with a visit to Bugbay. Gene accompanied her taking the gift of a white sheet to the Chief showing she had a good heart toward him and his people. That gentleman was sick with chicken pox, but he sat on the porch wrapped in his robes and gave a lengthy address welcoming the return of their first missionary, then another one (nearly as long) to welcome the new missionary. The crowd was large and the service beautiful, however six and a half hours round trip walking brought the ladies back to the Mission utterly exhausted. Gladys declared.

"I have never walked on or climbed over so many

tree trunks and fallen logs on one trip!" Tenderfoot Gene went to bed for awhile with sore muscles and blistered feet.

When the first of May came without word from Allan and Rosetta, Gladys fasted two days for her son and his wife. Two weeks later, a long, sweet letter came, and they wrote regularly after that.

The mud and thatch duplex for the teachers progressed slowly while the villages need of the Gospel nibbled on her heart. It was a glad day when she was free again to reach for those souls back in the jungles who did not know Jesus. She went. Every trip was singularly blest, but the aftermath was the same—total exhaustion.

"I don't know why it's taking so long to get back in shape," she wondered to Gene, "I've done a lot of this, though I felt worn out afterward, a little rest and I was o.k."

Now, it seemed to take longer to recover after each trip. One of her legs began to swell painfully whenever she walked. She tried to ignore the hurting and made jokes about her "ol lame leg." Early in June, her discomfort was so obvious, the missionaries insisted she see the Dutch Doctor who worked at the mine hospital.

"Mrs. Robinson, you have a tumor," he said, I suggest you return to the States for surgery and treatment. Immediately!"

A slap on her face could not have shocked her more.

"But, doctor, she faltered," I've just returned from the States—less than three months ago."

She wanted more time and while he doubted the wisdom of delay, the doctor agreed to check again in two weeks. Gladys speedily sent requests for urgent prayer and fasting to family, friends and church officials. She did not want to leave and hoped for the miracle that would allow her to stay, well and able to continue the work she loved. But God's inexplicable Will decreed otherwise.

Although the second examination showed no improvement, Gladys was still reluctant about going home. The doctor was blunt, "Mrs. Robinson, I suspect malignancy."

When Mission Officials heard the verdict, they ordered her home at once. She went, leaving her heart and most of her personal possessions confident she would soon return to Africa.

The doctor's suspicion was confirmed by surgery in America that revealed the fatal extent of the cancer invading her body.

She found even the darkest valley has a fragrant bloom or the ripple of a tiny refreshing stream. Gladys and Leo were not divorced. When he heard she was home ill, he came to be with her and renewed his vows to both her and the Lord. Their unexpected reunion, approved by those who loved her, brought a bitter-sweet happiness.

They made plans, in spite of the shadow. If and when the miracle came, Leo would go with her to Africa. He could take over the building and repairs and she would never again be alone on jungle trails. In the meantime, he was a constant friend and helper.

For a while she thought perhaps the path might wind upwards out of the valley. She refused to return to the hospital when the downward turn was evident. The old determined spirit asserted, "I'll not leave my family with hospital bills to pay when I'm gone, if Jesus does not see fit to heal me."

Those who cared stood helplessly by as she suffered and slowly retreated into the shadows of the valley. She hovered in a remote dimension past the need of conventional spiritual props that troubled Mary Wallace, wife of J. O., Glenn's brother. She was always kind, "Just a short scripture, dear." or "Make the prayer brief, if you don't mind."

"Was this the lady whose tremendous labors for God impressed the whole fellowship?"

Mary wondered, but did not share her questions with anyone.

E. L. Freeman, on furlough, visited Gladys in November 1953. She spoke wistfully of the miracle that would let her return to Bomi Hills. There could have been one, for there have been many such miracles, but the frail candle that flamed so brillantly and with such compassion in gross darkness was flickering down to the end of the wick in God's will.

A month later, December the 10th, one moment inexorable pain traced its haggard etching on her face, the next, a valiant spirit took wings and in that split second sudden glory illuminated with rare beauty the empty house of clay. The lingering sprinkle of eternity's golden sand awed the beholders, Marie, Glenn, Carmen, Norman, Leo, Louise Dugan, Mary Wallace and others. Her triumphant lifeless smile answered Mary, "The training drill is necessary preparation for combat, however when the grim battle rages, there is nothing to do but fight! She was a soldier who has just heard the Great Commander say "Well done!"

Goodbye Gladys!

Goodbye, until morning——that morning without clouds.

Nona Freeman

1. Gladys Robinson and her daughter, Marie, Apostolic Bible College, 1946.

2. Mrs. J. W. Wallace, (pastor's wife), Mrs. L. H. Hardwick (L. A. Leader) and Gladys Robinson at West Nashville Pentecostal Church, 1945.

3. A boat ride in front of the mission.

4. "Robbie" and "Reggie" sitting on a deserted bug-a-bug hill.

5. Pouring water from the water-vine for Moses.

6. Gladys with her friends in Liberia.

7. Missionary to Liberia, 1949.

8. Home in Bomi Hills.

9. Sister Robinson, Jean Barley, Brother and Sister J. T. Pugh and Brother and Sister A. T. Morgan, Port Arthur, Texas.

10. Gladys and her friend, Louise Dugan, Nashville, Tennessee, 1952.